Live Paleo Style

Overcome The Ancestral-Modern Mismatch
to Regain Your Natural Wellbeing

MIKI BEN-DOR (PH.D.)

To my wife, Lea, whose love and wisdom found
their way to every corner of this book and my life.

TABLE OF CONTENTS

How to read the book

The structure of the book aims to please the impatient reader. There is a summary of the book and the various chapters. Unlike other books, summaries appear at the beginning of the book and the chapters. It leaves the reader with the option to go or not to go deeper into the chapter's subject.

A Brief Summary of the Book

Not long ago, humans were hunter-gatherers wandering in a natural environment. Now, we live in a completely different modern world with a set of genes that evolved during the preceding two and a half million years. The premise of this book is that humans will function optimally under conditions in which their genetic inventory has evolved over millions of years. On the other hand, they will suffer from adjustment problems if forced to live in different conditions.

If we understand and become aware of the implications of this mismatch, the way to reduce suffering is paved before us.

Here are the main characteristics of the primal humans in their natural life and in their modern counterparts:

1. **Living in a small and stable group** - the primal human lived in groups of 15-50 who have known each other since birth. The level of interpersonal trust was maximal. In fact, a person rarely encountered people he did not know and whose interests differed from his own. Today

we live in huge frameworks such as cities, states, and the globe, and in many cases depend on the decisions of people who do not know us and whom we do not know.

2. **Most of the time was spent together** - Even sleep was a group activity, and there was a lot of mutual care for the children. Presently, many of us live away from traditional support systems.

3. **Sharing** - Sharing food was one of the primary norms in hunter-gatherer groups. Sharing meant that none of the group members were hungry when other members were satiated. Usually, the hunter did not participate in the division of the hunt to avoid the appearance of their relatives' preferences. Thus, no group member has ever seen another member abandoned to a state of hunger. Today personal ownership of property is sacred and homeless people do not get a second look.

4. **Equality** - There were no crowned leaders, and good hunters did not receive preferential treatment. Today inequality is the main engine behind the capitalist system and is accepted as natural.

5. **Autonomy** - No person could tell the other what to do, and no one owned the other's time. Even parents tended not to tell their children what to do. Everything was done voluntarily and out of a sense of belonging and commitment to the group. Today we operate in a series of hierarchical structures, in the family, at work, and in the state, where we are constantly fulfilling privileged people's demands.

. . . .

6. **No work** – There was no commitment to work at certain hours and places. No repetitive tasks were performed for hours, and the final product of each task was visible and consumed or used immediately. Today we sell our time to produce a product that we usually do not see to completion.

7. **The tasks were short-term and easy to achieve** - there was no long-term planning. There was no need for perseverance in performing a task over time. Today, many tasks require long-term persistence.

8. **Lots of free time** - Obtaining food only took a few hours, and plenty of time was left in the day to spend with the group. Today's work day, including the commute, requires most daylight hours and often even some evening hours.

9. **Nomadism** - Nomadism was a form of diversity, and nomadism made it possible to switch groups to solve interpersonal tension. Today we are economically invested in one place, so even if the immediate environment is stressful or unpleasant, it is difficult to change.

10. **Natural environment** – The natural environment had no noise or pollution.

11. **The risks were known and given** - the simple lifestyle meant that the dangers were known, and so were the ways to reduce them. Today, rapid technological progress causes us to expect to be able to eliminate every risk. Facing uncertainty is a source of frustration and stress.

. . . .

12. **Authenticity** - In the absence of work and in a state of perfect acquaintance with the group, there is no need to present a persona that is not authentic. Today we must show different personas in various social circumstances.

Continuous emotional stress results from the mismatch between our situation now and during most of our evolution. What can we do to help reduce some of that stress? Here are some suggestions, some easier and some more difficult to implement:

1. **Recognize and get to know your hunter-gatherer's core.** Recognizing the source of anxiety and stress in the mismatch between our innate core and modern reality is the basic condition for relief. In most cases, you will be able to find your own ways to relieve anxiety and stress if you recognize their source.

2. **Cultivate a small, stable community** – Sometimes, family and close friends feel a little 'boring.' Try to overcome that feeling. Privacy is overrated. Share your life with others. There is a lot of value in steady, trusted, intimate companions.

3. **Cultivate equality and autonomy** – True for marriage or any other close relationship. People close to you stay close if they feel equal and free to develop their potential. In fact, you will feel better among equals.

4. **Walk, ride, and travel in natural environments** – Moving in natural environments was as basic as breathing to hunter-gatherers.

5. **Find activities with immediate results** – Learn a language, help other people.

6. **Be spontaneous, just for the sake of it**. Spontaneity is an expression of autonomy and is often associated with activities that bring immediate results.

7. **Step away from large, hierarchical systems** – Working in certain large organizations, such as the government and the army, is not for everyone.

8. **Accept fate and uncertainty** – In many cases, stress is caused by circumstances that can't be changed.

9. **Don't feel ashamed when you crave free time**.

10. **Be authentic**. Don't be afraid to expose vulnerability. Authenticity is attractive.

11. **Eat evolutionary-matched foods**.

This book suggests early retirement and other behavioral and conceptual changes to overcome the emotional and physical mismatch. Some lucky people truly love their work, and some unlucky ones are economically unable to retire. Most of the measures that are recommended in the book can be taken without the need to retire.

Let's dive into the details of the mismatch and how its results can be minimized.

INTRODUCTION

PARADISE

A tropical island. The branches of the coconut tree descend into the azure water. This is the paradise where I first saw Adam. On the white sand, an orange spot flickered, a small fire on which he and his two friends had fried a fish they had just caught. At the end of the meal, they return to the camp where they live with sixteen men, women, and children. In the large hut where they spend their free time together, Adam lies on a bed with his youngest son. They lay hugged for a long time, motionless. Later, friends from a neighboring camp come to visit. The visitors sit down at the feet of each of the host men in a naked, long hug. The friends' conversation did not stop for a moment. No one was in a hurry to get anywhere. No one seems richer or poorer than his friend. If there was a visual expression of a deep, continuous sense of happiness, I saw it in Adam.

Adam's ancestors came to this island, Little Andaman, about sixty thousand years ago from Africa.

The Indian government, to which the Andaman Islands belong, banned the entry of Indian residents to the island. The group members managed to maintain their original way of life, living only tens of miles away from a modern settlement.

Watch the documentary 'The Lost Tribes of Andaman'. Still, even if you do not watch the video, you meet Adam if you are attentive to his presence. In fact, you have probably already met him without knowing it was him. You met him because parts of his personality are within you. The genes that determine your emotional reactions to the present reality evolved over two and a half million years under similar conditions to those of Adam. The change that has taken place in single genes in the ten-thousand years since we left his way of life and turned to an agricultural-industrial path is minimal.

Scientific evidence shows that the body is designed to feed on hunter-gatherers' food. We are also designed to feel comfortable in their lifestyle - In small, autonomous, and egalitarian groups that share the hunt and in which human dignity is the main law. Contrary to popular belief, we come from happy ancestors.

Can we return to paradise?

It will not, of course, be the same paradise. The technological wheel, represented by the agricultural, industrial, communications, and information revolutions, is impossible to reverse and does not need to be.

What will the post-industrial paradise look like then?

. . . .

- It will not have jobs in the industrial sense. It will not have hierarchical systems in which most perform only a small and specialized section of the production process.

- It will allow physical and mental leisure to create and maintain meaningful emotional and intellectual relationships with family, friends, and other interesting people.

- It will be possible to learn new and enriching topics, engage in sports, and often travel to beautiful and interesting places.

- It will have more equality. We will not feel inferior to our peers, nor will we feel superior to them.

- It will have complete financial and personal autonomy.

- It will not include pain or discomfort due to illness.

Once we have defined paradise, we must examine what changes are required to get closer to these characteristics.

And here's a little confession: I retired at 52 quite a few years ago, and I feel my life has not been far from this utopia.

I ceased to be involved in a commercial or industrial system. I research and write about topics that interest me. This is, if you will, a job, but not a job in the conventional sense of selling time and effort for monetary consideration. I dedicate about eight to twelve hours daily to this activity out of free choice. I have more mental energy to devote to my family. I study new subjects and engage in my

. . . .

favorite sports whenever I desire. I travel abroad several times yearly and do not feel financially dependent on anyone.

Yes, it's hard to believe, but I could have 'snuck' into paradise without anyone noticing.

KNOWLEDGE AND AWARENESS

In the following chapters, I will detail the components of the modern paradise and how readers can try to sneak into it with the help of courage and thinking.

The solution offered in this book is deeply personal. There is no intention to fix the world but the life of the individual in it.

Our urge to win and control the environment with the help of culture and technology causes us to confront the evolutionary basis that makes us up as individuals. Evolution is a mechanism of integration into the environment, while civilization is a mechanism of environmental control. This struggle between the evolutionary self and the cultural-technological self is the factor that envelops us in constant unease.

In the biblical story of the Garden of Eden, the tree of knowledge would impart "the knowledge of good and evil". However, the initial effect of eating from the tree was different. "Then the eyes of both of them were opened, and they realized they were naked". The authors of the Bible thought that the initial effect of acquiring knowledge was the acquisition of self-awareness.

The classification of things as good and evil, right or wrong, is not genetically inherent. It is mostly an application of cultural rules instilled in us by all the educators of culture - parents, teachers, social pressure, and mass communication. Before developing high self-awareness, the classification of good and evil closes the mind. Heightened self-awareness opens the mind. High self-awareness makes us realize how naked we are under the tops and makeup that culture has put on us.

The formation of a developed self-awareness means the celebration of this nudity. The celebration of the ability to re-examine the meaning given to us by culture. The celebration of our right and our ability to create our own meaning.

Developing a high level of self-awareness allows us to remove the weights of good and evil from our eyelids and see an amazing and challenging world awaiting our exploration.

This book is a journey to develop self-awareness in an original way, combining hundreds of thousands of years old knowledge with knowledge from the forefront of classical philosophical thought.

Developed self-awareness is an essential tool in trying to return to paradise. It makes it possible to distinguish between authentic insights and the limiting ideological burden we carry on our backs since birth.

....

Once a high level of self-awareness is acquired, it is time to apply the insights that this awareness provides. This book also tries to offer tools to help cross the wide river that flows between the acquisition of understanding and the act of change.

CULTURE - WORK - IDENTITY

Cultured behavior can be seen as a phenomenon of self-domestication. Along with the agricultural revolution, we inevitably had to domesticate ourselves. To give the constant attention necessary to breeding animals and plants, we had to adapt ourselves to our work discipline and suppress our natural desires.

For our own sake, in addition to the physical structures, we have also created virtual cultural arrangements within which we are supposed to live safely.

Work is such a structure that stands firmly at the center of the existence of human society. How did it happen that in biblical times, labor was a punishment (for eating from the tree of knowledge), and now it defines most of us?

Creating a new life and even a new identity after retiring is an inevitable transition from a working human's reality to a retiring human's existence. In this unique situation, we need all possible help. So, let's meet Adam, who will help us along the way.

ADAM

Adam, whom we met at the beginning of the book, became the most significant guide in my life, a compass that guides me in moments of doubt.

Using a compass that points to the north does not indicate an intention to reach the North Pole. The compass shows the north as the reference point, making it possible to find our way, even if it is to the south.

The reference point is provided by Adam with credibility, like that of a gyroscope. Defining Adam as the best guide you should know may be puzzling, but when you finish reading the book, you will know him well and recognize his full value.

The agricultural revolution, which began about ten thousand years ago, ripped our ancestors from the lifestyle they were evolutionarily adapted to.

The perception that the agricultural revolution was a positive turning point in human history was doubted by several thinkers. Jared Diamond, who wrote The Third Chimpanzee, Guns Germs and Steel, and Collapse, wrote that agriculture was "The worst mistake in the history of the human race". In the last ten thousand years, we went through the agricultural, industrial, and, most recently, the information revolution. However, the biological structure of our body remained largely the same as Adam's. Modern humans accelerate and bypass the slow evolutionary physical process by adopting culture.

The change required in our behavior to maintain a modern lifestyle is recorded in our minds as software. It is passed down from generation to generation. In this way, it bypasses the biological-genetic system. There are people in tribes neighboring Adam's tribe on other islands in the Andaman. They have become completely Western and study and work with the same proficiency as their Indian neighbors.

In hunter-gatherer societies, interpersonal relationships are face-to-face and intimate, lasting from infancy to old age. The modern world is a world of life in growing cities, increasing inequality and social alienation.

This fundamental change in interpersonal relationships is responsible for mental damages that make the psychologist more urgent and vital than the physician.

At the biological level, the food we eat - a meager variety of industrially processed foods - causes a series of diseases defined by experts as civilization diseases - diabetes, cancer, heart disease, autoimmune diseases, Alzheimer's, Parkinson's, and more.

This book will help locate the passages in which we have deviated from Adam's way of life by describing the inconsistency between the genetic and cultural dictates. It will also try to outline a direction for possible correction.

It is important to emphasize that there is no recommendation here for a sweeping waiver of the material supply of the Western world. Moreover, the technology and the high standard of living that follows are what enable us today to return to paradise under improved conditions.

. . . .

I have no idea what that beautiful son of the Onga tribe is called. Still, I feel I know him well after years of studying and thinking about him and his fellow human species members in the two and a half million years of their existence. Many times, he answered my questions even before I asked them. He is the compass, and he is the conscience. I feel his physical presence, with which I strive to connect. To connect with him, one must know him without the labels attached to him by modern human culture.

The Primal Human as a Model for Life in Paradise

To summarize

- The primal human was happy.

- The primal human is an excellent reference point for identifying cultural, physiological, and psychological pressure points at odds with our genetic base.

- The primal human lived:

  - In environmental conditions very different from ours.

    - With a lower sense of uncertainty.

    - In a smaller physical area.

  - Having perfect knowledge for survival.

  - Without seeing people in difficult situations without support.

....

- ○ According to rules established within his group by people he knew well.
- ○ Without an army and bureaucracy.
- The primal human could satisfy his needs with a reasonable effort in a few hours a day.
- The primal human had high degrees of equality and personal autonomy.

What can we do?

- Pay attention to the following:
  - ○ Water quality, air quality, light-dark differences, noise level, level of visual interest, eating times, and sleeping times.
- Organize the following:
  - ○ Physical activity with a purpose, an emotional support network, daily conversations with friends, joint projects, the possibility of moving between groups, opportunities for spontaneity, and diversity in everyday experience.
- Cultivate achievable aspirations.
- Accept risk and uncertainty as part of the reality of life.
- Check if you have responsibility, enthusiasm, challenge, friendship, love, trust, security, and a sense of involvement.

One day I asked a friend, an urbanite in body and soul, how she imagined paradise if she could build it. Her answer was:

- Friends - only those I love and know closely.

- A defined living space – no exposure to distant troubles and occurrences.

- Not spending most of our time indoor – being outside, by the sea, and in the sun.

- No cooking - gathering from what is available.

- Intellectual stimulation.

As we shall see, she accurately described the living conditions of the hunter-gatherer.

Throughout the following chapters, Adam will accompany us as a compass to increase awareness of our situation and the corrections necessary to reach a fulfilling life. This chapter will clarify the relevance of his world, the hunter-gatherer world, to our world. The importance of Adam as a faithful compass is closely related to a phenomenon not at all intuitive, although scientifically proven in various fields, the phenomenon of relativity in our lives. The need to adopt the paleo style compass stems partly from feeling insecure in a world without absoluteness, in a relative world.

Common characteristics of hunter-gatherer societies

In the second half of the twentieth century, anthropologists and social thinkers began to recognize the special positive side of the 'primitives' and their ability to be a model for the basic human condition. Richard Lee, the editor of the Cambridge Encyclopedia of Hunters and Gatherers, writes: "The world of hunting and gathering people .... represents the oldest and perhaps most successful human adaptation. Until about 12,000 years ago, virtually all humans lived as hunters and gatherers". Richard Lee attributes the descriptions of the wild, uncultured savage that lies beyond the fence of civilization to the settlers who thus justified his removal from lands they coveted for themselves.

Despite the great diversity of hunter-gatherer societies described in the encyclopedia, Richard Lee finds some of the most positive characteristics common to all:

1. They lived until recently without discipline dictated by an outside body to their small group.

2. They live in small groups without a central authority, armies, or bureaucracy.

3. They live together peacefully, solving their problems independently, without needing authority.

4. They can provide for their food and other needs, using limited stone, bone, wood, and fiber without needing much physical energy.

5. They have lived for thousands of years in one area without destroying their environment.

A common characteristic of hunter-gatherer societies is the group. A small, nomadic group usually contains between 15 and 50 individuals. These groups have several similar features, regardless of the area in which they live:

1. Equality - Leadership, if it exists, is less formal and more open to majority opinion than in rural societies. Leadership is done by setting an example, not by imperative. The leader can persuade but not dictate.

2. Nomadism and Mobility - Hunter-gatherers tend to move their camps frequently, and mobility is an important element in their politics. People in hunter-gatherer societies tend to "vote with their feet" to move to another camp when they are dissatisfied with the group members. Mobility is also an important means of resolving internal conflicts in a way that is almost impossible for sedentary residents.

3. Fission and fusion - Hunter-gatherer societies all tend to disperse in some seasons into small groups and unite in other seasons into larger groups.

4. Common land ownership - A particular area usually belongs to an extended family group. Still, reciprocity laws allow everyone to use the regions of other families.

Hunter-gatherer societies, scattered in different parts of the world, have a remarkably similar view of life:

1. The custom of sharing without compensation for the prey bounty is extremely central to the social interaction

of hunter-gatherers. Sharing in the prey is maintained with piety by encouraging behavior and social sanctions.

2. In most hunter-gatherer societies, there is a reference to the environment as a donor, giver, and enabler. The natural environment is their spiritual home, the source of all good things, and their lives are intertwined with the rest of nature. This view contradicts the agricultural/industrial belief that nature is a source of maximum utilization.

Living in a relative world

Everything is relative, said Albert Einstein, and he received a Nobel Prize. Einstein referred to physical forces in the universe and proved that even time is relative.

It can be shown quite easily that everything around us is relative.

Take, for example, the use of language. We live through language, think mostly through language, and experience most of what happens to us through language. The linguist Ferdinand de Saussure stated close to Einstein's time that the meaning we attach to each word is also relative. These words are scattered over a field of meaning (semantic field) and do not exist as absolute values. They take on precise meaning solely in relation to other words.

Let us analyze a very common word like 'good'. One may ask how good is 'good'?

Although we are not immediately aware of it when we choose to use the word, it is easy to prove that the word 'good' cannot be accurate without comparing words like 'excellent,' 'amazing,' 'okay,' and 'bad.' The term 'good' gets a more precise meaning only when you place it between 'amazing' and 'okay.' The same diagnosis also applies to nouns. Take a simple object like a 'book.' Even a word, seemingly non-valuable, needs words like 'notebook,' 'volume,' 'booklet,' and 'journal' to be accurately positioned in the relative space of the language.

Emotions, attitudes, and behaviors we experience daily are also relative. Love is an emotion whose relativity is easy to explain. Motherly love, spouse love, and brotherly love are all feelings of love, but they are relative. Without being aware, we place each of them synchronously on many relative axes, including an axis of concern, an axis of reciprocity, and an axis of sexual desire.

The lack of absoluteness of things causes us constant discomfort, and we expend energy trying to place daily occurrences on a relative scale.

Therefore, we are attracted like butterflies to what seems to be stable. Religion is probably the most common anchor of stability. Religions require their believers to accept several absolute rules and assumptions. Believers are happy to take the yoke of the commandments to return to a stable point where they can attribute all the relative things of their lives and significantly reduce uncertainty. The religious commandments themselves are islands of certainty in a sea of relativity. The typical arbitrariness of the commandments prevents them from being placed on a relative axis.

"Give me a lever long enough and a fulcrum on which to place it, and I shall move the earth", Archimedes said. Similarly, it can be said: "Give me a point of reference, and complications will become clear."

The primal, natural human can serve as such a reference point.

While still a student, I noticed that many differences between men and women could be explained by the differences between the hunter man and the gatherer woman (although women do hunt). The better sense of navigation in men, the greater social capacity of women, and their talent for locating things hidden in the fridge are good examples.

The primal human is suitable as a reference point to identify the cultural pressure points and the genetic sources for their existence. Using natural humans as a model can outline directions but does not require a return to the original state. Life will be more pleasant as we decrease the mental gaps between those conditions under which we were shaped by evolutionary selection.

In many cases, it is the use of modern technologies that creates conditions closer to the original human. We do not have the same natural food today. For example, agricultural produce is cultivated on lands that have long since lost many available minerals. Thus, today there is no choice but to rely to one degree or another on artificially produced supplements.

THE HUNTER-GATHERER - A CULTURE

Weston Price, an American Professor of Dentistry, traveled from 1930 to 1936 to numerous tribes living in pre-industrial conditions on remote corners of the globe. His goal was to learn how to prevent tooth decay. He visited the Aborigines in Australia, indigenous groups in the Torres Islands, islands in the Pacific Ocean, Africa, Alaska, and the Americas. Most of the tribes he visited lived in both pre-industrial and pre-agricultural conditions. His book Nutrition and Physical Degeneration summarized his six years of travels and research in these words: "It can be said quite accurately that among the tribes we dealt with, there is no begging, no paid prostitution, very little serious drunkenness, and surprisingly little crime at all, while everyone has enough to eat, enough to wear and housing appropriate to the standards of primitive natives. In what modern society can the same be said?"

Alongside the lack of adverse health effects, Price noted: "The happiness of these people in their homes and community life is striking and impressive wherever we have visited. I heard a quote from a white miner who spent twenty years in Uganda, who said that if he could have the paradise of his choice, where he would spend all eternity, it would be to live in Uganda as the natives of Uganda lived before modern civilization came to it." About the inhabitants of the islands of the Torres Straits between Australia and Papua New Guinea, Price writes:

"It would be difficult to find a more happy and contented people than the primitives in the Torres Strait Islands as

. . . .

they lived without contact with modern civilization. Indeed, they seem to resent the modern intrusion very acutely. They have nearly perfect bodies and associated personalities and characters of a high degree of excellence. One is continually impressed with the happiness, peace, and health in their friendly presence. These people are not lazy, but they do not struggle hard to obtain food. Necessities that are not readily at hand they do not have".

Price was just one of many ethnographers who have studied the living conditions of native groups and were deeply impressed by the high level of mental and physical health of the people we call primitive.

The wealth and happiness of Adam

Canadian anthropologist Richard Lee is one of the most quoted anthropologists about hunter-gatherer groups. Lee researched the Sun tribe, hunter-gatherers living on the edge of the Kalahari Desert in Namibia, and reported that they 'work' about two hours a day to obtain food. They play with their children, visit friends, or sit idly by most of the time. Similar reports have been received from anthropologists, who have studied dozens of hunter-gatherer tribes in the last century.

Richard Lee reports that a woman picks up enough food in one day to feed her family for three days and spends the rest of her time resting in camp, embroidering, visiting other camps, or hosting visitors from other camps. Cooking, cracking nuts, collecting firewood, and fetching water took about an hour to three hours of her time. In women, this regular work and recreation cycle is maintained throughout the year. Male hunters work more often than females but in a more irregular pattern. It is not uncommon for a hunter to hunt continuously for a week and then not hunt at all for two or three weeks. Since hunting is an activity that brings irregular returns, hunters sometimes experience a period of bad luck and stop hunting for a month or more. During these periods, visits, hospitality, and dancing are the main activities of man.

Marshall Sahlins calls the hunter-gatherers' way of living 'The Original Affluent Society'. Not all anthropologists accept all of his findings, but they are generally sound. They may have been even more significant during the Paleolithic period when large prey animals were more abundant.

Sahlins claims that the original affluent society was none other than that of the hunter - in which all the material desires of the people were easily satisfied. The current problem lies with the wants, not the means. He writes: "To assert that the hunters are affluent is to deny then that the human condition is an ordained tragedy, with man the prisoner at hard labor of a perpetual disparity between his unlimited wants and his insufficient means".

Sahlins quotes Sir George Gray, governor of Southwest Australia, writing in 1841 about the Aborigines of his area: "But in his own district a native is very differently situated; he knows exactly what it produces, the proper time at which the several articles are in season, and the readiest means of procuring them. According to these circumstances he regulates his visits to different portions of his hunting ground; and I can only say that I have always found the greatest abundance in their huts."

On the Kung in the Kalahari Desert, Sahlins quotes Marshall, an anthropologist who studied them in the late 1950s: "they were comparatively free from material pressures. …they all had what they needed or could make what they needed, for every man can and does make the things that men make and every woman the things that women make. …. They lived in a kind of material plenty".

To emphasize the insignificance of material assets in hunting groups, Sahlins brings the testimony of a westerner who met the Bushmen in the early 1950s:

"This matter of presents gave us many an anxious moment. We were humiliated by the realization of how little there was we could give to the Bushmen. Almost everything seemed unlikely to make life smoother. They themselves had practically no possessions: a loin strap, a skin blanket and a leather satchel. There was nothing that they could not assemble in one minute, wrap up in their blankets and carry on their shoulders for a journey of a thousand miles. They had no sense of possession."

Sahlins adds that it is not that the hunter-gatherers are curbing their material desire; they just never built it.

Thus, one can add the evidence of sharing in nomadic hunter-gatherer groups and conclude that humans evolved without the lust to accumulate property.

The same is true of work. The primal human life did not require hard work, and the contradictions with the work values of the contemporary world could not be more direct.

On the attitude of the Indians in America to work, Sahlins quotes Gusinde, who wrote: "the Yámana are not capable of continuous, daily hard labor, much to the chagrin of European farmers and employers for whom they often work. Their work is more a matter of fits and starts. In these occasional efforts, they can develop considerable energy for a certain time. After that, however, they show a desire for an incalculably long rest period during which they lie about doing nothing without showing great fatigue."

The economy of abundance that Marshall Sahlins describes is completely opposite to the economy of Adam Smith, the philosophical father of the economics of the industrial world. Adam Smith's economic theory assumes that we live in perpetual scarcity and a perpetual desire for more and more things. This assumption is made effective through tremendous advertising mechanisms, whose function is to create in our minds a shortage that will cause us to consume. Imagine a world without advertising. Take, for example, the decline in clothing spending that would have occurred if fashion had not changed in each of the four seasons. In general, the whole fashion mechanism- in clothing, furniture, cars, or faucets, the very reason for its existence and promotion is to bring us to consume more. Without external manipulation of our minds, we do not want more and more things.

. . . .

How can we understand a world without markets and no prices, a world where there is no shortage, and why is it important to understand a world so far away from us?

The answer is that this world is not far from us at all, and it is as close as can be - it dwells within us; it is in our genes.

Rhythm differences between culture and genetics

Most people accept that humans evolved from monkeys, and 99% of our genes are identical to the chimpanzee and the bonobo. However, the regulation of the genes' expression also changed.

In the last seven million years, two main conspicuous changes between the chimpanzee and us appeared:

1. We became bipedal (stood and walked on two legs) about six million years ago.
2. About three hundred thousand years ago, our brain volume completed a two million years increase to almost four times the brain size of a chimpanzee.

For 99.6% of the two and a half million years of our evolution, we lived as hunter-gatherers and only 0.4% of the time (about ten thousand years) as farmers and city dwellers.

The fact that we can survive and reproduce rapidly is evidence of man's incredible adaptability by cultural means, relative to other animals. This capability has a price tag, however. We must adapt to modern life culturally, having mental abilities shaped over millions of years to cope with a band of about 30 hunter-gatherers moving in a pristine natural environment.

Environmental Deviation (Bio Deviation)

Being in different environmental conditions from the original adaptation is not unique to humans. It often happens in nature and is the engine of evolution. This phenomenon has been defined by a scientist named Stephen Boyden as Biodeviation.

A unique aspect of this process in humans is their high intellectual ability to adapt to changing conditions.

Boyden has compiled a list of areas in which we live in deviations from the hunter-gatherers' base.

He notes that the hunter-gatherers' activities provided them with an object for a significant intellectual challenge. They had an opportunity to combine in-depth knowledge of flora and fauna with the utilization of natural physical ability and an opportunity to demonstrate courage and interpersonal cooperation in performing a meaningful task for the group. The payoff for success was immediate, both in obtaining food and appreciation gestures

Boyden further notes that members of hunter-gatherer groups chose to sleep when they felt the need to do so, usually in the afternoon and evening. In addition to hunting, gathering, and sleeping, group members spent significant time producing tools for hunting or processing materials such as wood, bone, or leather, as well as producing ornaments. Some specialized in storytelling or making music.

According to Boyden, the primal human spent a lot of time daily discussing issues of common interest, exchanging information about the environment, discussing problems and personal concerns, and telling stories and jokes. The approach to educating children was usually permissive, and the mother had personal responsibility for raising her children. The other women also took part in caring for the children. The generation gap was not pronounced, although the elderly enjoyed a special prestige.

Despite the suspicious treatment of foreigners, excessive violence between groups is not one of the salient features of pre-agricultural societies.

Boyden adds that the environment was always a focus of interest, and there was a sense of harmony between its various components, including humans. Diversity was experienced through the differences between day and night and from season to season.

The main cause of death was infection following an injury while hunting or other physical activity or death by a predator. Viral and bacterial infections or starvation were not the common causes of death.

Boyden enumerates the deviations from these living conditions as we experience them today. Among the physical components in which the environment differs today are the following:

- Water quality is relatively poor (chlorine and other pollutants, lack of minerals).

- Poor air quality.

- Extended exposure to light.

- Relatively high noise levels.

- An environment with low visual interest.

- Food is in a higher quantity than what our body is built for.

- Lack of free time for mid-day naps.

- Lack of frequent, goal-directed, varied physical activity intensity.

On the level of emotional deficiencies relative to the world of hunter-gatherers, he enumerates:

- Lack of support networks.

- Reduction in opportunities for frequent dialogue with friends, extended family, and the group on common issues.

- Lack of meaningful interactions between members and short-term, joint projects.

- Fewer options for switching to another group. The alternative is living in isolation.

- Disrupting the balance between an environment with a high degree of interest and an overly rapid pace of change.

- Fewer opportunities for spontaneity in actions and behaviors and diversity in daily experience.

. . . .

- The disappearance of short-term goals and aspirations that can be fulfilled in a short time.

Anxiety, risk, and uncertainty

Boyden refrained from addressing a major problem that stems from the difference between our living conditions and genetic makeup. That is the diversity of psychopathologies and especially anxiety disorders nowadays. The source of anxiety disorders is likely the gap between our ancestors' perception of risk versus uncertainty, two similar but different concepts.

Risk is an independent statistic - the probability that something desirable will not happen or, using positive wording of the phenomenon - a chance - the likelihood that something positive will happen.

Uncertainty is an element that can be reduced with the help of knowledge. The more we invest in reducing uncertainty, the closer we get to the game of chance - statistical risk.

A good example of the difference between risk and uncertainty can be found in weather forecasting. Much is done to reduce weather uncertainty: studying thermodynamics, setting up satellite weather tracking systems, and developing computer models for weather forecasts. These do not change the probability that it will rain on a certain day in a certain place.

Although he knew less of how the world works, it is conceivable that the primal human felt less uncertainty than we do.

We can accept risk as a natural fact. Because we cannot control risk, we have learned throughout evolution not to let its existence affect our mental health.

An important cause of anxiety is the element of uncertainty, which we seemingly can influence. Anxiety seems to have evolved to motivate us to deal with uncertainty. The relative simplicity of primal human life is why he encountered fewer uncertain situations:

- The geographic area to which the primal human referred was relatively limited and was familiar to him. Nowadays, the area we are referring to is huge. Today 'the world is your oyster'. Through television, for example, we are constantly shown catastrophes in faraway places.

- The number of people referred to by the primal human was small and familiar to him from childhood.

  Nowadays, the number of people we refer to is huge. Green organizations tell us that our wasteful and polluting behavior is "endangering the existence of the human species". We are expected to treat the billions of people on the planet as members of our group. We meet quite a few people who don't know us. Their non-personal attitude toward us may affect us, especially when we need their permission to do or obtain something. Family and best friends are equivalent in our lives to a group in the life of the primal human. The daily contact

. . . .

with everyone else can add uncertainty and, consequently, emotional stress.

- The needs of primal humans were limited to food and shelter.

    Nowadays, the number of needs is enormous and, accordingly, the amount and complexity of the decisions that need to be made. Any such decision exposes us to uncertainty. Are we purchasing the right washing machine? Is the plan offered by the phone company suitable for us? Hundreds of decisions are made under conditions of uncertainty. There is no way to understand and learn all the variables involved in every decision. There is no way to reduce the uncertainty to a level we are genetically engineered to deal with.

- Knowledge of flora and fauna, and its availability as food, was perfect.

    Nowadays, knowledge about our food is outsourced to experts whose main motive is profit, not our health.

- The primal human did not have the technology to know more.

    Nowadays, we know that knowledge exists somewhere. We could compare the different phone plans if we had the time and patience. The gap between the theoretical ability to lower the level of uncertainty and the lack of this ability in practice is a widespread source of frustration.

- The life experience of the primal humans was such that anyone they knew could sustain themselves at the level of full satisfaction of their basic needs. The group supported the sick and the weak without any expectation of return. The primal humans had never met poor or neglected people, so they had no reason to fear that this might also be their fate.

Nowadays, life experience includes awareness of a series of catastrophes. So that we do not forget that poverty can also be close to home, the poverty report is published every year.

We know from descriptions of people who lived in hunter-gatherer societies that their main perceived risks are snakes, predators, and other large animals. The main risk is life itself and not their standard of living or quality of life.

Risk is perceived by modern society as technological backwardness. Over the last ten thousand years, the entire human project can be described as an attempt to gain control of factors previously considered subject to risk. Domestication of animals and plants was the first step. Instead of going on a hunting trip and returning empty-handed, agriculture has increased the probability of success. But part of the price is a complex world with more opportunities to be exposed to uncertainty.

THE PRIMAL HUMAN IN OUR MINDS - EVOLUTIONARY PSYCHOLOGY

After a hundred years of interpreting our psychic life according to Freud's psychology, many scientists can now lay solid scientific foundations for studying the mind.

In his book How the Brain Works, Stephen Pinker discusses several studies on identical twins. They shared traits such as IQ, neuroticism, introversion, writing, and math abilities. They also held the same opinions about the death penalty, apartheid, career choices, hobbies, religious commitment, and the ideal character of spouses.

Furthermore, identical twins that were raised separately were similar even in very specific characteristics, such as non-participation in elections, compulsive counting, and volunteering to become firefighters.

Evolutionary psychology claims that just as our eyes, hands, feet, and ears evolved, so did our mental faculties. The mind is not some supreme being, subject to physiological laws but a system of messages that pass through the brain's predetermined modules. Each module evolved for millions of years to help us address the specific problems and challenges we faced in our hunting and gathering lives.

Psychology thus becomes a reverse engineering exercise with questions such as "For what purpose did anxiety evolve?" and "What is the survival benefit of depression?".

At the clinical level, this approach looks for solutions that differ from Freud's. No more endless probing into parent-child relationships in early childhood but an attempt to understand why an evolutionary mechanism, designed to benefit us, has gone awry and how it can be corrected.

In her book 'Naked Soul,' Prof. Ada Lampert gives an example of anorexia. The classic psychoanalytic explanation is an acute tension between the parents of the anorexia patient. Lampert offers two possible evolutionary reasons for the phenomenon: one assumes an unconscious desire to delay fertility in respect of an elder non-childbearing sister, a known behavior in other animals, and a second explanation, which recognizes that anorexia may serve to prevent adolescent pregnancy by delaying fertility.

This scientific approach contributes greatly to the usefulness of primitive humans as a model. It leads to the recognition that alongside physical organs in our body, the more covert aspects of human behavior are also dictated by the brain.

According to Pinker, brain modules must use several environmental assumptions to solve complex problems. The solution that the brain provides is a kind of equation solution with several unknowns. Without assumptions, the number of possible solutions would have exceeded the brain's ability to process them. Some beliefs are genetically inherent in our brains and contradict our current reality.

Other scientists use the primal human as a model and achieve good results in their field.

Stephen Ilardi, a professor at the University of Kansas, specializes in treating clinical depression. He argues that several causes of clinical depression involve deviating from a lifestyle our brains have adapted to for millions of years. Humans developed a series of behaviors intended to prevent them from entering a state of depression, a condition which for a primal human meant death. According to him, humans would not have continued to exist had they not developed these behaviors. The biggest deviation between our lifestyle and that of the primal human is the quantity and quality of social contact.

According to Ilardi, humans are accustomed to continuous social contact, and members of the hunter-gatherer group are rarely alone. Ilardi contrasts this way of life with the current lifestyle in which we are alone for long periods. He cites the Amish as an example of a cohesive community with no cases of depression.

From this analysis and the results of further studies, Ilardi formulated a clinical depression treatment plan that he claims is more effective than antidepressants. The program has six components that aim to bring our modern lifestyle closer to that of primal humans:

. . . .

1. Exercise - A study conducted at Duke University found that 35 minutes of aerobic exercise, three times a week, is equal to, and even exceeds, the results of taking antidepressants.

2. Omega-3 oil - The relative amount of Omega-3 that the primal human consumed exceeds several times today's level. Studies have shown that Omega-3s help combats depression. Ilardi recommends taking an Omega-3 supplement containing one gram of EPA per day.

3. Exposure to daylight - We spend most of our time in enclosed spaces in light conditions lacking the quality and quantity of natural light. Reduced exposure to sunlight (especially in winter) is known to cause a type of depression called SAD. Dr. Ilardi recommends a minimum of 30 minutes of daily exposure to daylight or special lamps that mimic daylight.

4. Preventive Negative Reflection Strategy – Prevalence of negative thoughts, a common phenomenon among those suffering from depression. Ilardi recommends activities to stop these thoughts, like calling a friend, exercising, and writing.

5. Social Support - Loneliness is a cause of depression, and depression encourages staying in solitude. Ilardi recommends spending as much time as possible with friends and family.

6. Sleep - Sleep deprivation is one of the main risk factors for depression. The primal humans were exposed to strong daylight, replaced by complete darkness. These

radical changes regulated the production of hormones that allow for about 8 hours of sleep. Today, this contrast is almost non-existent. Ilardi recommends going to bed and getting up at the same hours every day, wearing pajamas, dimming lights, turning off a TV and computer, reading in bed, and avoiding caffeine and alcohol a few hours before bed.

As you can see, most of the program's components apply to all of us, even if we are not depressed.

Another psychological condition, which can be better understood as a modern manifestation of hunting psychology, is the syndrome known as Attention Deficit Disorder (ADD). In his book Attention 'Deficit Disorder - A Different Perspective', Thom Hartmann hypothesizes that people with Attention Deficit Hyperactivity Disorder (ADHD) are hunters who have fallen into the modern world. He lists a series of attention deficit disorder characteristics. He shows how those traits can cause a disadvantage in an agricultural/industrial situation and an advantage in a hunter-gatherer situation. From the perspective of a person with attention deficit disorder:

- Being easily distracted is a disadvantage in an industrial mode but an advantage in hunter mode. The ability to quickly enter a chase of prey without preparation is advantageous.

- A hunter lacks planning ability, is disorganized, and is impulsive (a disadvantage in industrial mode). However, he is flexible and willing to change strategy quickly, which is an advantage in hunter mode.

. . . .

- Lack of awareness of how long it will take to perform a task is a disadvantage in industrial mode. Still, high stamina and perseverance in achieving a visible goal is an advantage in the hunter mode.

- Impatience is a disadvantage in the industrial mode. Still, results orientation and an awareness of distance from the target are an advantage for the hunter.

- The inability to follow instructions is an obstacle in industrial mode but not hunter mode.

- Impulsivity, acting without considering the consequences, is a major problem in the industrial mode. However, willingness and ability to take risks and face danger are essential in hunter mode.

Hartman suggests that people with ADHD, or 'hunters,' find an occupation that suits their character.

It is also interesting to note that Hartman raised his hypotheses several decades ago before genes responsible for ADHD were identified. A study by Dan Eisenberg among a Kenyan tribe (Ariaal), some still living as nomads and some as permanent residents, confirms Hartmann's hypothesis. He found that individuals with unique genes for ADHD (DRD4 / 7R) are more successful in nomadic conditions but have difficulty meeting their needs when living a sedentary lifestyle.

Using the Primal Human as a Model Does Not negate the Achievements of Human Culture

Using the primal human as a model may suggest a value judgment regarding modern humans. This is not the intention. Moreover, the ability of all of us to adapt our behavior to such radically different conditions is a wonder. The conduct of the primal human may, at times, be reflected in a more positive light to identify the direction of a proposed change.

Another possibly perceived value judgment is of culture as an elite conspiracy. Culture can indeed be interpreted as a successful attempt by the strong to exploit the weak. Even if such an interpretation is sometimes correct, it does not mean that the powerful, throughout all cultural generations, have been or currently are bad people. They certainly do not sit in global conspiracy meetings and discuss ways to increase repression to raise their profits. We are all carried in the strong current of the capitalist system. The game's rules have been defined since the dawn of the days of the agricultural revolution. People cannot act differently without completely renouncing the standard of living and the way of life to which they are accustomed. Attempting to change towards anarchy will result in the extermination of most humans. The attempt at communism by Russia caused considerable damage to a large group of people when it was fortunately dismantled.

. . . .

At the same time, this does not mean that the capitalist system should remain in its raw version. Measures of happiness are highest in Scandinavian countries that have not given up the capitalist system but allow relatively high individual economic autonomy alongside somewhat higher equality.

The Ego and Me

To summarize

- The ego is the presented 'I' It is necessary nowadays when the number, diversity, and complexity of social interactions require the presentation of a changing and diverse self.

- The ego is an expensive component to maintain, both financially and emotionally.

- There is no need for such a developed ego after retirement.

- We have been prepared for work for years; however, we must prepare ourselves for retirement.

- Preparing ourselves for a non-working life involves designing a new me.

- Buddhism and postmodernism offer a more flexible approach to the 'I'.

What can we do?

- Acknowledge the constant change that the 'I' goes through. Learn to be aware of cultural demands in the 'I'.

- Reduce the ego after retirement – it is expensive to maintain and is not as useful as it was when working

- Shame and pride are feelings cultivated by culture as a means of self-discipline. Try to reduce their influence on you.

- Reveal your weaknesses to the right extent and at the right time.

- Replace being insulted with listening and understanding.

- Be sensitive to society's response while minimizing the need for approval.

In his book Collapse, Jared Diamond describes the Easter Islands as one of the most isolated places on earth. Captain Cook, who arrived at the islands in 1767, saw from a few miles the huge stone-sculptures of the pointed human figures, wearing the round hat, that adorned the island's towering fringes. When he arrived, the meager tens of hungry-looking island inhabitants eagerly awaited him. Diamond tells the story of the island's ecological collapse sometime before Cook's arrival. From a record population of 5,000 people, the island deteriorated in about two hundred years to the state in which Cook found it. The huge statues, placed on family stages, were erected as a symbol of the power of the family. So the sculptures became increasingly enormous over time as each family tried to surpass its neighbor. Diamond claims the process was stopped only with the extinction of the special palm trees used to quarry the stones (inserting wedges and wetting them) and transporting the sculptures from the quarrying site to the placement site. The island's economy collapsed because the fishing boats were also made from those trees.

Some question the correctness of Diamond's historical description and attribute the collapse of the Easter Island economy to the genocide later committed by the white man. Either way, the huge stone sculptures of the Easter Islands clearly glorify the 'I,' as were the pyramids in Egypt and many other similar structures.

WHO AM I?

Trying to define our 'I' for ourselves will quickly become impossible. Where exactly does this 'I' reside? What does it include? What gives us the feeling of a character with a continuous history to whom things happen and who uniquely responds to them? Does the 'I' exist in relation to society? Maybe the 'I' is in the sum of our qualities?

The more we try to deepen and put our finger on the 'I,' the more it will become clear to us that the 'I' is an amorphous body. This experience becomes even more impossible when entering the dimension of time. Is the self of today the same as the self of my childhood? Of yesterday's I?

. . . .

The Portuguese poet Fernando Pessoa dealt extensively with identifying and abolishing the 'I.' In 'The Book of Disquiet', he writes: 'God with whom am I present? How much am I? Who am I? What is this space between you and me? ' Pessoa points to the strange fact that we can think about our 'self' outside the self. If so, who is the I who think of the 'I'?

Pessoa concludes that the 'I' is hollow. He writes: "And I, I really, am the center that does not exist except through the geometry of the abyss. I am the nothingness around which this movement revolves ... I am a well without walls, but with the mists of the walls, the center of everything around its nothingness".

In contrast to the difficulty of defining our 'self' to ourselves, it will not be difficult to describe who we are to others. If we work, the first thing that will define us to others will probably be the profession. Sadly, this is the level of detail most people interested in who we are will want to know. The job is our identity for most of the day, for most of the year, and for most of our lives. Most of our externally and internally perceived successes and failures lie in the professional part of our identity.

The gap between the difficulty in defining the 'I' for us and the ease of expressing it for others reveals one of the major problems of retiring.

As long as we work, we also adopt the professional definition of 'I' for ourselves. We believe we know who we are. When retirement from work confronts us with losing that significant component of identity, the sense of 'I' remains empty.

THE EGO

Another baggage we have accumulated over our lives is that component of the 'I' called ego. Today, ego means self-worth or extroverted self-worth. "He has a big ego" is said of someone who expects others to give his presence a respectable place or someone who seems confident in himself and demonstrates it.

Our use here of ego will therefore refer to the presented part of the 'I,' the ego that makes sure that we appear in life in a way that will help us survive. In other words, unlike the self, which sometimes changes passively in response to social changes, the ego is actively adapted to life situations.

It is difficult to draw the boundary between the 'I' and the ego. The need for this differentiation intensifies during the transition between work and retirement.

In a state of superficial acquaintance, we do not tend to appreciate a person who does not respect himself. The development of the ego, the 'I' presented, is thus a necessary means of receiving appreciation from others in a state of superficial acquaintance.

The range of behaviors we are required to adopt today is extremely wide. While the primal human may have needed to display an ego towards strangers when they rarely met, we need countless behaviors tailored to relationship status, hierarchy differences, and media. We adopt different behaviors and use different language in the family, at work, in front of bureaucracy, and in a store. We behave differently at work towards subordinates, associates, and superiors. We subconsciously choose dozens or hundreds of times a day, the appropriate behavior for each unique combination of place/situation/hierarchy/means of communication.

In this complex situation, there is an essential need for the existence of the 'I' presented, which on the one hand, is distinct from the other and, on the other hand, can be designed as required. There is no resemblance between the 'I' we adopt in our family to the self we present to our superiors. The need for an ego suit is low in the family, and we can be soft, warm, and forgiving. In front of our subordinates at work, we are considerate and decisive. In contrast, in front of our superiors, we are loyal. In every interaction out of the daily dozens, we suppress parts inappropriate to the situation and emphasize or play other aspects of our personality. In conclusion, ego development is necessary to survive in a complex reality like ours.

The ego, a survival tool, limits the capacity for personal development. As mentioned, guarding our image is a task we are taught from childhood. The ban on showing weakness towards strangers and the ability to present the right character in the right place is meticulously nurtured by our parents.

No wonder most men talk to each other about worldly issues rather than personal and interpersonal issues. God forbid they may reveal weakness. Who knows when this

. . . .

liability exposure will be exploited against them in the competitive world where they earn their livelihood.

Presenting objects is one of the most effective ways to build the ego shield. A car, a house, and clothes are great aids in delivering the sturdy 'I.' The thought of getting to a meeting with friends in a less luxurious car can ruin our desire to meet them. In almost every decision regarding the product or service we consume, we consider the implications of the thing on our public 'self'. No wonder watches are a major tool in class broadcasting. They are easy to carry and are always on display. The 'I' demonstration displayed is basically the sole purpose of jewelry.

It is not surprising, then, that jewelry was rare in archaeological sites before social hierarchy and the complexity of social interaction appeared.

Maintaining the ego comes with emotional and financial effort. Therefore, to make connecting to the authentic self easier, a narrow and shrunken ego is the most important and useful asset the retiree can acquire.

The economic value of a limited ego is substantial, and its emotional weight (or rather its absence) is invaluable. The retiree, who has excluded himself from the competition of existence, does not need a well-developed and nurtured ego. A smaller ego saves the emotional strength and the money required for maintenance while at work.

Any parent or sibling to more than one child can attest that we are different from birth. Genetic diversity is important for survival as it maintains a pool of genes available for adaptation to external change and is present in every species. The genetic structure is unique to us and is the basis of the 'I.' Our sense of I would have been much weaker if we were all completely identical in our qualities and abilities.

The identity of each of us is created from recognizing our diversity as compared to others. Personality tests examine patterns of thinking, emotions, and behavior and rank people in traits such as aggression, propensity for introversion, sentimentality, and the like. We all have all the attributes but at different levels. Linguist Ferdinand de Saussure has shown that words have meaning only in relation to other words. In the same manner, identities can only be a relative thing. Renowned psychiatrist and psychoanalyst Donald Winnicott stated that our identity appears when it is reflected to us by the other. Thus, in any specific social composition, our 'I' resonates differently. Even according to Winnicott, the 'I' is not as stable and unambiguous as we think.

Another source of identity dynamics is environmental-cultural. Opinions about the relative importance of the environment versus genetics vary. Still, no doubt if there is room for change; it is here. A respectable element in our decisions is the desire to get our parents' approval. Hundreds of parental and cultural social orders fill our to-do list and form part of our identity.

Buddhism and postmodernism teach us the possibility of a less sacred and more flexible reference to the self. The sense of 'I' exists, and there is no real possibility of ignoring it. On the other hand, you should consider accepting easily and sometimes encouraging the changes the 'I' undergoes.

We are not the same person we were when we were kids, and we are not the same person we were yesterday. Time and life events leave a mark on us and change us.

Over time, personality tests on large populations show a change in personality throughout the life cycle. For example, one of the characteristics of these tests is Agreeableness - the degree to which a person needs a cordial relationship with others. This characteristic increases continuously with age. Studies find that the sharpest increase in the need for satisfying relationships with others occurs between the ages of 45 and 55.

Another characteristic exacerbated at 45 to 55 is 'Openness To Experience', the degree to which a person needs intellectual stimulation, change, and diversity.

The Adoption of a small ego identity

The transition to non-work is such a fundamental change that it justifies the cessation of autopilot use and re-examining of the whole ego issue. We are no longer dependent on others for our livelihood. Is there any justification for maintaining the precious protective suit called 'ego' at the same level?

The preoccupation with the 'I' and the 'ego' is a counter-reaction to the growing loss of autonomy in the industrial age. The enormous increase in the amount and variety of interpersonal interactions is typical of the industrial-technological era.

The involvement of large and impersonal systems (workplace, bureaucracy) in setting our agenda obliges us to present a coherent identity. The study of the self became a branch of science – psychology.

Because work is such an important component of our identity, we have virtually no choice but to shape a new identity for ourselves upon retirement. Economic autonomy will make us consider less and less what others expect of us. Minimizing this dependence also includes aspects of financial savings.

In general, it can be said that the importance of status symbols in our lives will decrease. At first, we will still wear good clothes when we go out into the public space. Still, slowly we will feel less need to dress smartly. However, we certainly do not want to stand out conspicuously and defiantly (or maybe we do?).

The central theme for changing the 'I,' and with it the ego, for suiting a state of non-work is the degree of internalization of family and cultural expectations acquired at another time for the purpose of integration into the world of work.

How to change? Identify and re-examine every culturally internalized requirement and decide whether to keep or throw it into the basket of history according to its usefulness in the new situation.

The first step in such an examination is to locate behaviors that stem from a desire to satisfy the expectations of others. This is not about compiling a list. The goal is to develop an ongoing ability to observe and question ingrained worldviews. A condition for developing this ability is not to take any established truth for granted.

EXAMINING THE VALIDITY OF SOCIAL ORDERS THROUGH LANGUAGE

There are four ways to create a sculpture: remove pieces from a lump of material, shape it from a plastic material, mold it into a mold or paste material additions layer by layer. The formation of the 'I' can be likened to dynamic sculpturing, using every method all the time. There are parts of the 'I' with which we are born and which we remove (suppress). Plastic parts of our personality adapt elements that are molded into a uniform social pattern that sets clear boundaries and adds personal experiences.

The stacking image seems best suited to address the layers of social expectations. Ideology, the system of ideas that society labels right, weaves into language and clings invisibly as a transparent glue to words. The words are perceived by us as a neutral representation of the things they are supposed to represent. But a word is never a neutral thing. The word takes on additional meaning according to the ideology of the society in which we live.

Words like 'security,' 'homeland,' 'blood,' 'discipline,' 'liberty,' and 'victory' are prominent words that not only signify the concept but are imbued with a heavy ideological burden. Let's take a simple noun like 'book.' The word 'book' does not just describe a thick notebook containing printed words that combine a coherent idea.

Exploiting the ideological emotional charge of words is done when trying to change the mind of another. We encounter ideology through language without noticing it. As any advertising person will tell you - the hidden way is the effective way.

We have a natural, instinctive resistance to being dictated by others. The hidden ideological nature of language secures obedience. The ideology is implemented by giving positive or negative meanings to words. We must constantly examine the transparent ideological glue, the words.

A change requires putting all the words in quotes, identifying and separating them as much as possible from their ideological baggage, and discussing them without having a valuable meaning in the first place.

Let us apply the Buddhist principle of abolishing desires to words. The word 'work' will then lose the positive connotation of creation, diligence, and existence. It will remain only an accurate description of the occupation of producing something for someone else to make money. In contrast, the word 'idleness' will lose the meaning of evading effort and will only become a description of a situation in which something purposeful is not done. When not working, very few greenhouse gases and other pollutants are produced. When you do not work, you do not earn money that allows you to buy more and more products and services, which also causes negative environmental effects. We may conclude that there are also some positive aspects to a state of idleness.

Reinventing ourselves

Sometimes because of fear of the unknown, we ignore the change that is happening or should happen in our personality. Failure to accept the need for change means not facing reality as it is. Reality is constantly changing, and so are we. Sometimes, fighting change or ignoring it means exposing ourselves to a huge and powerful wave of truth. The more we persist in our resistance, the more the water that pushes us will collect and thus will require more and more effort from us to maintain resistance. We are all afraid of change to one degree or another, and we all, as a defense mechanism, repress reality to some degree.

Retiring from work, the pillar of our identity, we need to reinvent ourselves.

We have been prepared for work through the whole education system. We have been given decades to gain experience and form our working identity.

In retirement, we face a situation where no one has bothered to train us. Creating a new identity requires independent work when the page of our lives is everything but clean. This is not an easy task, but it is also an opportunity.

Many times, what we define as society's expectations exist only in our minds. Examining these expectations' existence, validity, applicability, and value to your current situation may be the most interesting and rewarding engagement during retirement.

TRAINING IN THE DESIGN OF THE 'I'

In psychological therapy, awareness of the problem is the key to change. Buddhism, on the other hand, adds practice (meditation) as a way of change.

Identifying the ideological baggage of words and the impact of society's expectations on our behavior are issues that require daily attention to embark on lasting freedom. To realize the change, you should add practice to them, as we will see below.

We must accept and forgive ourselves for our weaknesses and minimize our pride in our strong qualities. Like our weaknesses, our talents are cards dealt to us. In fact, there is no difference between having pride in being beautiful and having pride in being smart.

Do not shy from expositions of vulnerability. Try to deliberately expose others to cases from the 'corner of failures,' i.e., issues in which you failed or your weaknesses arose. You will be surprised to find that if the exposure is done in the right measure and context, it will lead to appreciation instead of the contempt you would expect. The absence of the need to hide weaknesses or failures indicates self-confidence and mental resilience.

But even if you come across contempt, focus on ignoring its insulting effect as part of the training. A contempt response often stems from the respondent's inner difficulty meeting an intolerable part within himself, which we happen to reflect.

Acknowledging our weaknesses and accepting them without shame or guilt, alongside true modesty, will help develop closer and more authentic interpersonal connections. It is a way of exposing the human we have built. This exposure allows others to break free from the need to present in front of us a perfect self, thus creating a relaxed mutual atmosphere. This recognition will also enable us to accept the failures that await each of us.

Shame and pride are tools culture develops to ensure the self-application of cultural discipline. Shame is the punishment we punish ourselves for violating commands, and pride is the reward we give ourselves for successfully functioning under orders.

Minimizing feelings of shame and pride is a necessary step toward directing our behavior, not according to the commands and expectations of others.

If we do not demand ourselves to be who others want us to be, we do not need to demonstrate our successes to them. The need to be proud of our accomplishments or talents is a sign that we have not been freed from the expectations of others.

An important measure of success in the ego minimization process is the test of insult. Insult is an emotional response to what others say. It is especially strong if the insults relate to the substances we try to hide. Retirement from work may be interpreted as laziness, inability, and evasion of responsibility.

. . . .

Insult in response to such interpretations indicates the need for further work on ego reduction through self-forgiveness and optimal minimization of arrogance.

The insult can be replaced with an understanding of the other's reaction. Those close to us, who do not understand our motives and choose to stick labels on us, sometimes do so in response to anxiety. A person who acts contrary to social expectations threatens the system of values that holds our life together.

There is not, and probably never will be, a human without external approval. Winnicott said, "there is no baby without a mother". We are social animals, and a demonstrated lack of need for social acceptance will make it difficult for others to communicate with us. Again, it's all a matter of timing and measure. The answer should be given by each of us according to the circumstances of his life. The less the need for approval, the higher the level of autonomy.

Equality, Autonomy, and Culture

To summarize

- Equality was always a necessary, existential element in primal societies.

- Equality in food distribution is a prominent and clear characteristic of hunter-gatherer groups.

- A sense of immediacy and the unimportance of the future and the past led to a feeling of independence and personal autonomy.

- Equality and autonomy are most likely central psychological needs with a genetic basis.

- Our current world is based on inequality as a fundamental catalyst of the capitalist drive. At the same time, personal autonomy decreases as our control over nature increases.

- Culture bypasses the slow rate of genetic changes by changing human behavior through extra-physiological means.

- The price of culture, which results from the will to control, is the need to be a loyal servant of its rules.

- The intolerance of culture to non-uniformity among its members leads to a loss of autonomy.

- The ideology - a broken walking cane designed to achieve compliance.

- Primitivism - the negation of time, language, number, and art.

- Postmodernism reaches a similar conclusion to primitivism in denying the universal truth of any ideology.

- The 'I' is also a type of ideology.

- Technology leads to alienation.

- The character of language as an ideological device.

- Postmodern awareness paves the way for a return to a way of life free of ideologies better matching human biological-psychic design.

WHAT CAN WE DO?

- Reduce preoccupation with the future to the minimum necessary.

- Increase spontaneity to feel a sense of autonomy.

- Identify the areas where autonomous expression is possible.

- Doubt all ideologies.

- Locate the language mines that encourage compliance.

- Locate the culture's gripping points on our identity.

- Reunite with the world by freeing yourself from the passions and aversions that culture has instilled in us.

- Building a subjective sense of equality and autonomy is necessary for healthy and proper functioning in society and the family. Equality allows us to dream, and autonomy will enable us to perform.

EQUALITY

"It is evening time. The three hunters return to the camp. On their shoulders is a deer they managed to hunt after two days of stalking. The camp children gather around them, rejoicing. The adults stay in their huts. The hunters instruct the children to bring their parent's dishes, and thus a line of empty plates is arranged around the deer.

On the skin the hunters have stripped, they put the pieces of meat, and in a suitable container, they put the inner parts. The portions are evenly and meticulously distributed between the dishes before them. Everybody in the camp is busy roasting and consuming the meat". In these words, an anthropologist described a typical distribution of game meat in a society of hunter-gatherers.

In most cases, the hunter himself is forbidden to participate in the distribution of the meat. The portioning of the flesh by the hunter would create a sense of ownership and impair the group's equality.

The equality among hunter-gatherer tribes has garnered much research attention from anthropologists. There is also some archaeological evidence for equality among nomadic groups throughout the pre-agricultural period. Among the evidence are the similar size of the residential units and the complete absence of luxury items.

Each member of the tribe, including women, knew how to make all the tools they needed. Accumulating property is impractical in nomadic conditions due to the difficulty of carrying heavy baggage to the next camp. In addition, in the absence of refrigeration, most foods also cannot be stored.

Thus, for millions of years, the human species lived in an environment where conditions that create inequality were extremely limited.

Today, however, inequality between individuals is a condition for the economic flourishing of human society, competition being the cornerstone of the capitalist system.

Inequality in society received the status of an ideology through the existence of the market as a mechanism that guarantees economic well-being. Market and specialization are based on inequality.

Inequality is what allows the talented to accumulate more.

We are trained from infancy to compete. Starting in first grade, we participate in exams ranking us relative to others. This is how we learn that competition is a natural attitude. We are brought up to accept that there are rich people as a fact of life.

EQUALITY IN HUNTER-GATHERER SOCIETIES

An interesting mechanism for maintaining a sense of equality among hunters with an unequal skill level is described by anthropologist Richard Lee. He reports on an expression of humor among the Sun tribe in Africa, whose whole purpose is to prevent the creation of pride in successful hunters:

A hunter from those who participated in the hunt but failed to kill an animal says: "This animal is much smaller than it seemed to me when it was in the thicket" his friend adds, "yes, it is really small; it was already not worth following the spur". The one who hunted the animal joins in and says, "yes, I think it isn't worth the effort to carry it at all ...."

The Members of the Ituri tribe in the Congo have received in-depth researched coverage, being hunter-gatherers who continue to this day in their traditional way of life, despite the presence of an agricultural environment in their immediate vicinity for many years. The two sub-tribes of the Itori - the Aka and the Efe live in different parts of a huge forest in the Congo and speak different languages. In both, as researcher Hideki Takashima describes, members of the tribe are not allowed to own property beyond what they need. If by chance, they accumulate property, they must give it away; otherwise, it will be confiscated. Lending clothing, hunting equipment, and utensils are also very common. All food brought to the camp is divided among the camp residents, and highly desirable food is evenly distributed very carefully. Particularly strong are the social norms regarding the distributive sharing of meat.

. . . .

Another issue about which there is cooperativeness is knowledge concerning existential actions. Each member of the Itori tribe has enough knowledge for self-sustenance. Although there are gaps in abilities and achievements, it is never mentioned and does not affect everyday life.

The issue of elephant hunting is a wonderful example of consciously maintaining the conditions for equality or, more accurately, the non-development of conditions for inequality. Hunting elephants is dangerous and requires a specialization that is not shared by all, even though they are all good hunters. Elephant hunting requires a great deal of knowledge of their behavior and ecology, courage, and hunting talent. Elephant hunters are called by a special name, *tuma*. All this does not mean they have a special status or additional authority in daily life. They never brag about their ability or courage and always remain modest when others praise their talent.

Prof. Nurit Byrd David, an Israeli researcher from the University of Haifa, has extensively researched the Nayaka tribe in the jungles of India. According to her reports, they maintain an equal distribution of large animals that have been hunted. They give objects without expectation of return. The Nayaka also make sure not to show special ties between family members in the same group other than the spouse. The closer the degree of family relations, the more restricted the rules of their interpersonal behavior. Beard David attributes this behavior to maintaining autonomy in an environment where intimacy is not great. Still, it can also be interpreted as a reluctance to cause discrimination

. . . .

between family members and non-family members within a small group.

Another anthropologist, Barbara Bodenhor, studies the Inupiaq tribe from northern Alaska and reports a very high level of personal autonomy in the tribe. No member of the group can tell others what to do. Everyone who helped in the hunt is entitled to a share of the catch, regardless of the quality or quantity of their contribution. Help is defined with an extremely relaxed approach, and even a good story is accepted as help that entitles an equal share of the loot. According to Eleanor Licock's research, the status of women in hunter-gatherer societies is a "separate but equal status". She prefers the use of autonomy over equality since women, she says, hold the power of decisions about their fate, similar to men. Female autonomy is achieved through equal access to means and resources. Other studies show that women who collect are not dependent on men for subsistence.

REASONS FOR EQUALITY IN HUNTER-GATHERER SOCIETIES

Several researchers explain the prevalence of cooperatives and equality in hunter-gatherer societies. Tim Ingold, a well-known researcher, emphasizes the approach to the hunted animals as common property. According to Ingold, the hunter feels that the animal he hunts belongs to everyone and must be shared. James Woodburn, another esteemed researcher, argues that the desire to avoid the harms of inequality dictates equal distribution. Nurit Byrd David emphasizes the self-perception of the hunter-gatherers as an integral part of the environment. They feel that their environment provides food for people as parents give food to children; therefore, it is natural to divide it equally.

The capitalist concepts of ownership and inequality, inherent in us from childhood, make it difficult for us to understand the way of thinking of people living in a world of concepts so different from ours. Wub-E-Ke-Niew, an Indian-American writer and thinker, is quoted as saying: "With us In the Ojibwa language, when you go to fetch water from the lake, you are not going to "take water", We say, "You're going to meet the lake".

Can we perceive a life experience in which we and the lake are participating entities along with many other equivalent entities, including animals and plants, in a process called life, all in a series of interactions in which the concept of ownership has no meaning?

THE DESIRE FOR EQUALITY IS INGRAINED IN OUR MINDS

A study published in Nature magazine examined the feeling of fairness in brown cappuccino monkeys.

Each monkey pair was initially given equal rewards for a similar task. After they learned the task, they were given unequal rewards for a similar effort. In the next stage, inequality worsened. One of the two monkeys received a more coveted reward even though it made no effort.

As long as they received equal rewards for equal effort, cooperation with the researchers was 95%. But when they realized they were given unequal rewards, their cooperation dropped to almost 50% of the trials.

When one of the monkeys received a more coveted reward without demonstrating effort, the cooperation rate dropped to 20%. The monkeys waived the reward out of protest.

The results show that these monkeys have expectations of social justice. According to the researchers, the study's results support an approach that claims humans have an evolutionary basis for aversion to unfairness.

A relic of the primordial need for equality can also be found in sports or games. Since these are voluntary activities, we are not willing to participate in or watch games that are not based on equality and fairness. The large sums of money recently invested in preventing drugs use in sports are proof of the vitality of providing equal opportunity for all participants in sports

AUTONOMY

THE NEED FOR CONTROL AND OUR LEVEL OF PERSONAL AUTONOMY

Our unique history is a history of gaining increasing control over our environment. Control began with the creation of tools from stone, wood, and bone, followed by the domestication of fire, animals, and the cultivation of edible plants. It continued with the production of copper and iron, developing machines for mass production, developing life-prolonging drugs, controlling information, and transferring it at the speed of light. All of this and scientific progress, in general, are evidence of the achievement of humans' increasing control over their lives.

Language also gives us a sense of control through the ability to call things by name.

Although the attainment of control has always been the result of a group effort, we still expect control over our life circumstances as individuals. This is why it is so difficult to accept that the level of control an individual has over his life circumstances is quite limited. "Why did god take him?" we ask when someone dies. For millions of years, God has constantly taken people of all ages, good and bad. To date, he has taken several billions of people, and there is still not one exception. And here we still are, frustrated by our lack of control. How is it that we, who sometimes control huge natural processes at the molecular level, still face diseases, accidents, and death?

The great paradox is that success in gaining increasing control over reality leads to a growing loss of our sense of autonomy as individuals. To increasingly control nature, we must organize ourselves into ever-increasing systems with an ever-increasing level of complexity. The more complex the system, the less deviation it tolerates. The individual plays a specialized role in these systems, a smaller and smaller screw whose criticality for the whole system grows continually. Individuals must forgo their autonomy for the system to function.

. . . .

An extreme example of the phenomenon of relinquishing personal autonomy to gain control is the military. The military is a large and complex organization whose whole essence is to achieve complete control. To fulfill its purpose, the individuals who serve (serve!) must give up every symbol of control. Uniforms and specific mandatory haircut styles eliminate any external expression of a unique, autonomous identity. Scheduled and all personal activities are subject to the organization's needs.

As we organize into larger groups: couples, families, groups, tribes, villages, towns, cities, countries, groups of countries, world, we need more and more rules. In addition, the more complex life is, the more rules we need. That is why Congress never stops enacting more and more laws. Every law restricts autonomy, and thus we are in an ongoing process of limiting autonomy.

Sweden is the only European country where hikers can set up a tent in any public space, not just in regulated campsites.

Similarly, we have forbidden thousands of other things, some only for the reason of "what if everyone did it?"

The need for complete control over our lives makes us controlled by the need. We spend our time in attempts at control and in constant frustration at our inability to control everything instead of enjoying what the world offers.

Autonomy in hunter-gatherer societies

There is no description of humans' temporary or continuous economic exploitation by other humans in nomadic hunter-gatherer societies.

Anthropologist Tim Ingold argues that the uniqueness of the hunter-gatherer is that it undermines the definitions of the concept of society in its modern sense. It shows us how to live socially without having to live in society.

There are several definitions of 'society,' some of which are contradictory. Some definitions refer to warmth, intimacy, close acquaintance, and trust. On the other hand, some definitions refer to society as an association of rational people united in a sense that stems from a common self-interest.

In the primary society, all the emotional components exist without the need for the contractual restrictions of the second part. Face-to-face relationships are the dominant feature of interpersonal relationships in hunter-gatherer societies. This characteristic disappears with the specialization and change of the social frameworks for the city and the state. An example of the level of social alienation we experience can be found in the hated encounter with the automatic switchboard, which completely replaced the human voice.

We lack face-to-face contact, not to mention years of close acquaintance with the variety of faces we encounter. Face-to-face with familiar faces - this was the main form of communication that the primal human knew.

Equality and cooperation in hunter-gatherer societies greatly impressed Marx and Hegel, constituted the model for communistic life, and claimed to be the natural model. It turns out that its large-scale implementation has led to the need for monstrous means of repression. In the absence of an interpersonal relationship, let alone a face-to-face relationship, repression was needed to force a redistribution of economic resources.

Hunter-gatherer groups do not usually maintain a fixed group composition, and there is a movement of people and guests. This flexible pattern allows for personal autonomy and paves the way for resolving tensions and interpersonal conflicts. Disengagement from the group for a few days and even more is actually considered legitimate.

Even if people are considered more talented in decision-making, they never force their opinion on the rest of the group. Leadership is not determined but occurs and is based solely on a belief in the leader's abilities and a belief in his unwillingness to use that trust to create an advantage or display arrogance.

IMMEDIACY AND AUTONOMY

One way to deal with the feeling of lack of control is to accept at least partially the Buddhist view that we should come to terms with the fact that we have no control. As we learn to eliminate the need for control, to accept reality not as good or bad but as it is, to embrace it and flow with it. Hunter-gatherers teach us additional ways.

According to Tim Ingold, there are three recurring concepts in studying hunter-gatherer societies: immediacy, autonomy, and cooperation. The three concepts are not separate components of hunter-gatherer life but are intertwined and derived from one another. The three concepts humans evolved over millions of years impact our lives today.

Immediacy exists in the supreme importance of the present, disregard for the future, and proximity to people and nature.

"One researcher after another", Ingold writes, "reported a lack of any level of forethought, especially on food issues". Marshall Sahlins defined it as "always oriented to the present".

Emphasis on the present leads to an increase in the sense of personal autonomy. There is no pressure to fulfill a future task. Failure to worry about the future leads to a lack of dependence on others. This is not to say that the relationships in the hunter-gatherer groups are cold and short. The memory of the close life together and especially the doing together is preserved. Thus the movement from group to a group can take place without fear.

The unplanned nature of spontaneity creates a sense of autonomy. Most of the activity of hunter-gatherers is spontaneous. Going out hunting is usually not a pre-planned activity, as are other activities like dancing or visiting friends. Part of the charm of spontaneity is offering a rare sense of autonomy.

. . . .

There is a contrast between the immediacy in time and geography between the primal human and us. Our lives are mediated by technology. We rarely meet the people we speak with in person, and we often communicate by delayed (text, email) rather than immediate means. We spend little time and energy thinking about the present versus the future and the past. The same is true in the context of the immediate proximity to nature. Not only are we not usually in nature, but nature itself is disappearing.

> *My wife and I used to spend most of our vacations cycling abroad. Stacking the little equipment we need on the bike, and pedaling from town to town. After staying in B & Bs several times, we decided to try camping. France was the first place we tried (10,000 camping sites.) We added a tent, air mattresses, sleeping bags, and cooking utensils to our bike equipment. Closeness to nature is difficult to buy with money.*

A high level of personal autonomy is a side effect of the immediacy of time resulting from a sense of economic freedom. A sense of financial independence is not necessarily the same as economic independence. According to Ingold, the autonomy of the primal human is different in nature from that of the cultural human. For us, autonomy means independence and privacy. The position is against society, as individuals compete for status and success. In primal humans, the level of cooperation is high, as well as the level of interdependence. Both characteristics do not impair the sense of personal autonomy, supported by a high level of mutual trust resulting from many years of close acquaintance. The prevailing principle is that a person's autonomy emanates from deep respect from peers.

Unsurprisingly, these are the cornerstones of a happy married life: cooperation, equality, and autonomy.

How is autonomy made possible in a situation where there is economic dependence? The answer is in the existence of a cultural mechanism that establishes support from the group regardless of the individual's contribution. This mechanism, in hunter-gatherer societies, is the cooperative mechanism.

The sharing phenomenon we previously discussed in different contexts is so prevalent in hunter-gatherer societies that researchers have suggested that the urge is innate. Others have indicated that cooperation is the invention that led to the creation of human society. Cooperation is the only way to maintain autonomy in the living conditions of hunter-gatherers. There is no debate about the economic benefit of cooperation in situations where hunting is of large animals and irregular. The cooperation makes it possible to balance the volatility in the hunting results without creating a dependence between one individual and another. Not seeing hunting as property acquisition is linked to not perceiving hunting as work but more as a natural interaction with the environment. Since the hunter has not invested work in the hunt, he does not expect a return.

One can perhaps see in today's fundraising activities the modern expression of the impulse to cooperate that originates in hunter-gatherer societies.

Richard Lee summarizes his discussion of communism in its natural version in a hunter-gatherer society: "It is a long experience of egalitarian sharing that has shaped our past. Although we have adopted the lives of hierarchical societies. The human species preserves deep-rooted equality, a deep-rooted commitment to the norm of reciprocity, and a deep-rooted passion for a sense of commonality. All theories of justice revolve around the same principles, and a sense of anger, seeing a violation of those principles, points to the depth of that attraction".

From the close connection described above between immediacy and autonomy emerges a method for creating temporary islands of autonomy in everyday life. Spontaneity and creativity are two approaches that have the potential to undermine the general anti-autonomous order dictated by culture. Spontaneity means challenging a schedule set by needs dictated by disciplined activity. Creativity brings about change in the conventional way things are done. Even simple daily activities like cooking can be a substrate for expressing autonomy through creativity. Typically, only day-to-day activities are possible topics for temporary pro-autonomous creativity. Long-term activities tend to be well monitored by the cultural apparatus (commercial, governmental, artistic). Therefore the chance of building autonomy is minimal.

. . . .

Another way to achieve temporary autonomy is through mental nomadism. This concept frequently appears in the context of web browsing. This way, freedom of movement can be maintained between discussion groups. The anonymity that characterizes the network adds to the sense of autonomy.

In this context, the retiree is exceptional in creating a permanent island of autonomy. Retirement allows us to regain the lost sense of autonomy by eliminating a central anti-autonomous cultural structure - work.

CULTURE

The word culture has a very broad meaning. Culture in this discussion is the accumulation of knowledge and changes in behaviors that have been added in the ten thousand years since the outbreak of the agricultural revolution. Human culture has enabled us to shorten the processes of adaptation to a changing environment, whether by changing the environment or our behavior. It is a unique mechanism that replaces the slow physiological evolutionary mechanism.

Genetic mutations often include suppressing genes that existed in the past but whose expression in new conditions interferes with survival. A good example is the suppression of the fur-growing gene, characteristic of our monkey relatives, making us the only primate without fur. Giving up coats allowed us to cool the body at the highest rate of all mammals and enabled us to move long distances.

Culture has oppressive characteristics. Like its genetic sister, culture also requires us to suppress behaviors our genes encourage.

The big difference between the other animals and us is that a suppressed gene ceases to be active in animals. In contrast, culture's suppressed motivations remain active, and only their external expressions are suppressed.

This phenomenon of two contradictory mechanisms within us has a mental price.

Freud called the phenomenon 'suppression of impulses'. The negative connotation of the word 'impulses' denies us the possibility of giving a legitimate place to those genetic tendencies.

Another problem with cultural survival mechanisms is that while evolution allows genetic variability between individuals, cultures usually have little tolerance for variance.

James Stephenson, a young architect from New York, spent about a year with a group of Hadza hunter-gatherers living on Lake Eyasi in Tanzania. In his book, The Language of the Land, Stephenson tells of a group member named Citoti. Citoti has characteristics that we would have diagnosed as paranoid. He set his seat at the top of a towering hill, from which he could observe the surroundings at any time and make sure that no one could approach and kill him. He's convinced his wife has bewitched him. Citoti is subject to bouts of energy and rage. He occasionally climbs a tree to its highest branches. He sends threats and curses at his friends while demonstrating to them with the help of a bow and arrow what he will do to them. This unusual behavior does not seem to bother his group mates, and they continue to treat him like any other group member. He is a full partner in all the activities. He is not discriminated against when distributing prey, even though he usually does not go hunting with the gang.

How different is this acceptance from our tendency to get the different and the injured out of sight?

The task of identifying justified behavioral variability rests with us as individuals. The proper procedure will involve identifying the discrepancy between the genetic and this cultural imperative and creating a personal way to solve it. This is the role assigned to the person striving for maximum autonomy.

FROM THE PRIMAL HUMAN TO POSTMODERNISM – THE CIRCLE CLOSES

What relevance does a modern philosophical thought like postmodernism have to a person trying to calibrate his life with the help of a model of a primal human?

Learning postmodern thinking can be both an exciting and depressing experience. Postmodernism is an approach that specializes in locating and eliminating sacred cows as well as analyzing the reasons why sacred cows should no longer be born. But you can, if you want, find in it an optimistic line. We are finally free to explore life in a way those cows will not block.

. . . .

As we will see below, there is a close connection between the postmodern views and the use of the primal human as a model for managing our lives.

THE DEATH OF IDEOLOGIES

In the late 1970s, the Quebec government commissioned the French philosopher Jean-François Lyotard a work that would analyze the impact of technology on the perception of the exact sciences.

Lyotard wrote a report attempting to answer a much broader question under Le Condition Postmodern - The postmodern situation. This report is considered a major milestone in the emergence of postmodern thought. To sum up Lyotard's message in one sentence, the postmodern state of mind is a state of suspicion and skepticism towards the existence of comprehensive and true ideology.

Culture can be seen as an ideology whose flag is inscribed in the letters PROGRESS. For those who want more autonomy, it is important to understand the postmodern message, which exposes the other side of progress. This message of postmodern times is the same as the primal ones, and this similarity doubles its validity.

The pursuit of authentic reality becomes urgent as we approach the end of our lives. The opportunity to identify the illusion of ideology is one of the more important enterprises of postmodernism. Ideology probably began no more than ten thousand years ago, together with the agricultural revolution. If you ask a hunter-gatherer about

. . . .

his ideology, he will not know what you are talking about. Even if you try to explain an ideology to him, he will still not understand what you are talking about. He has no ideology at all. The explicit definition of ideology is only necessary to ensure uniformity and discipline in a large group of people.

Hunter-gatherer groups lived for two million years without ideology. Yet, they did not destroy themselves and the world in which they lived.

Thus, postmodernism confronts us with ten thousand years of agricultural/industrial life under changing ideologies. We complete a full cycle and return to the initial state. There is no big story. Many 'big stories' only led to suffering and destruction - Communism, Nazism, radical Islam, radical Christianity, and radical Judaism. The purer the ideologies, the more damage they did.

For us, who are accustomed to living in an ideological framework, the fear of promiscuity is quite understandable.

Postmodernism is not an ideology. If anything, it is an anti-ideology in its quest not to take any truth for granted. Similarly, any opinion is considered a mere interpretation to be examined.

Interpretation is a basic activity of the mind, a central pillar in our unceasing efforts to understand the world. Whether an interpretation relies on an ideological infrastructure or independent thought structures, it will always be an interpretation, not the fact itself.

Part of the postmodern project diagnoses turned out to have been formulated before. It is said that Nietzsche was a forerunner of postmodernism. Still, it is possible to go back much further. In the sixth century BCE, a thinker known as the enlightened Buddha came to the same conclusion: The self is a construct and doesn't exist. We build it ourselves, and the sooner we get rid of it, the better.

Perhaps at first glance, the connection between the 'I' and ideology is unclear, but is the 'I' not our interpretation of our life story? - telling the story of our lives as if it is a structured development? Creating order out of disorder? Drawing a line along which we have flowed to this day and will continue to flow? For the continuous existence of such an ego, most people need a guideline, an interpretation that can be adhered to. Lyotard, "The loss of the great, ongoing story shatters the subject ('I') into heterogeneous moments of subjectivity that do not connect to the fit identity". In other words, without ideology, the 'I' is essentially a random collection of events. Interestingly, this fluidity of the self allows psychotherapists to question detrimental aspects of it.

In this sense, Buddha is even more extreme than the typical psychotherapist. He says that attempting to build a coherent identity is the source of suffering. To get to Nirvana, you must stop telling yourself this story. All is an interdependent complexity that is constantly changing. The desperate clinging to an ostensibly coherent storyline must lead to a situation where there is a contradiction between it and the changing life. The inevitable result is suffering. We can't tell what the degree of ego among hunter-gatherers was. Still, from the evidence of their happiness, we can deduce that they did not have to face the inevitable result

. . . .

the Buddha anticipated. They, thus, may have had a weak sense of self.

FERNANDO PESSOA, POSTMODERNISM AND THE SELF

The Portuguese poet Fernando Pessoa wrote much of his work under Heteronyms, imaginary characters with a whole life story and a cohesive set of views. In Pessoa, the heteronym writes in a style that suits his fictional personality. One of the main heteronyms, Alberto Cairo, is, in a sense, an anti-poet. Most poets saw their role as providers of interpretations of the environment they examined. According to the classical concept, the artist should provide a point of view that will illuminate a phenomenon in a new light. On the other hand, Cairo's writing explicitly rejects interpretation, and he reports only what his senses perceive.

Cairo writes:

Opening the window is not enough
to see the fields and the river,
It is not enough not to be blind
to see the trees and flowers.
You should also not have any philosophy.
Philosophy produces no trees, only ideas.
There is only each of us, like a cave.
There is only a closed window, and the whole world is outside:
And dream of what can be seen if the window opens,
that is never what is seen when the window opens.

. . . .

Pessoa (in the guise of Cairo) describes reality as it is seen through the eyes of a hunter-gatherer. His vision is primal, virgin vision. Philosophy, also a form of ideology and interpretation, prevents us from seeing things as they are. Philosophy is a cave (referring to Plato, who claimed that philosophy frees us from the cave). The attempt to adopt ideas beyond the visible things, as Plato recommends (the dream of what can be seen if the window is opened), is hopeless. It interferes with seeing things as they are.

The 'I' as an interpretation is also expressed by the existence of sixty different heteronyms in Pessoa. Alvaro de Campos, another Pessoa heteronym, says: "To be precise, Fernando Pessoa doesn't really exist."

Ideology, in its classical sense, as a guide to an explicit way of life, is the tying of life to one idea and one form of interpretation. It is, therefore, easy to identify an ideology by its unique language. Every aspect of life is tied to the ideology's preferred adjectives - chauvinist, bourgeois, communist, heretic, capitalist, socialist, nationalistic, holy, and pure. According to Pessoa, as the heteronym Cairo, the mere giving of an adjective to a natural thing is an interpretation. In another poem, he writes: "A day of rain is as beautiful as a day of sunshine. / Both exist each as it is".

Buddha formulates the same principle when applied to the human experience. At the same time, he points the way to a correct examination of the experience without desire or aversion - an observation free of all judgment. Defining something as attractive or repulsive is an interpretation. The religious order of Buddhism to detach from all interpretations is the equivalent of the methodological order of postmodernism.

POSTMODERNISM AS A BRIDGE TO THE PRIMACY

The postmodern enterprise is an enterprise of exposure and dissolution. The identification and discovery of the interpretive element lead to getting closer to the natural state of things before civilization appeared. The primal condition was devoid of ideology or interpretation. Proximity to nature, the unmediated connection with reality, the absence of complex social power structures, and high personal autonomy made ideology superfluous. In this sense, in its quest to dismantle ideologies, postmodernism marks the closing of a circle and the return to the primal way of experiencing reality.

One of the main phenomena that fuels the postmodern era is alienation. Humans become increasingly alienated from the urban/technological/commercial environment. What relevance does a modern philosophical thought like postmodernism have to a person trying to calibrate his life with the help of a model of a primal human?

As I said at the beginning of this chapter, practicing postmodern thinking can be both exciting and depressing. However, it allows us to question the necessity of the various ideas. It sets us free to explore life, removing those sacred cows that block our path.

. . . .

PRIMITIVISM

One of the primary goals of postmodern suspicion was the concept of 'progress' in its scientific and cultural context. Another group that does not define itself as postmodern but at the same time fundamentally undermines the validity of the concept of progress is a current called 'primitivism.'

'Primitivism' defines itself as anarchistic. That is, it denies the usefulness of a government of any kind. Primitivist thinkers advocate a return to the life patterns that existed before civilization. One should not be too impressed by the anarchist label they have given themselves. It apparently remains at the philosophical level. Their thinking is useful as a point of reference to understanding the fundamental, fateful change that constitutes the development of civilization.

The leading thinker of this current is John Zerzan. Zerzan analyzes the main manifestations of human deviation from his ancient sources. According to Zerzan, time, language, numbers, and art are the primary expressions of increasing alienation from nature. At the basis of these four expressions is the only cause for separation from nature - the division of labor. Without a division of labor or, in its other name - specialization - there is no economy. Specialization requires coordination between separate production stages and between production and the market. Zerzan argues that this coordination demanded the existence of the alienating factors - language, number, art, and time. What all four have in common is that they are symbolic tools and not the thing itself. By the way, postmodern thinkers also point to over-representativeness as a sign of alienation.

. . . .

Time is the first expression of alienation by Zerzan. Conceiving the time difference from the present requires looking at things from the outside. The thought of the past or the future requires disconnecting from the present. Both do not exist and therefore need cultural construction, 'construct' in the postmodern language, leading to alienation from the present.

According to Zerzan, language is a purely representative tool and a product of a society in alienation. The language was created to enable economy and control. It gives the individual a sense of power by calling things by name but is equally an effective tool, as already explained, for ideological control in particular.

A number symbol is also crucial for developing a cultural world. The process of counting, like the process of naming, is a process of gaining control. It is part of the process of domestication identified with the beginning of civilization. In hunter-gatherer languages, there are usually no names for numbers higher than three or four. We may see this as a sign of backwardness, but it can also be seen as a sign of freedom - the lack of need for control.

The fact that art, in the beginning, deals with matters of religion and sanctity testifies to its role - control. Art is the earliest form of ceremonial ideological expression. Control is an urgent need in a society where the division of labor necessarily leads to inequality. The return is always relative to the contribution, as Adam Smith mathematically proved. Inequality and specialization can lead to society's dissolution; religion and sacred art come to prevent this. Religion is a means of control, and art (including the ceremony) is its language.

REPRESENTATION

A parallel phenomenon associated with alienation is representativeness. Technology increases representation. Instead of the thing itself, we meet the representation of the item. Painting and photography are easy-to-identify means of representation. The voice emanating from the phone's earpiece is not the real thing but its representation. The same goes for all other technological means of communication.

Using a mediating, representative medium allows for the insertion of ideological bias easily and covertly. Greek paintings of gods and medieval religious paintings of the story of Jesus are one of the first examples of using a representative medium to add an ideological element to a message. Today it is clear that almost no representation does not come with the addition of ideology or manipulation. The examples are innumerable, from photoshopped faces of politicians or models through flag colors that dominate the image of politicians to choosing the journalists and interviewees that appear on media networks.

POSTMODERNISM – DESPAIR OR HOPE?

Cala Lassen, a thinker and social activist against the takeover of our lives by the world of advertising and corporations, sums up postmodern philosophy as the most oppressive philosophy that has ever emerged from the Western mind.

He says this philosophy means that we have reached an endpoint in human history: "The modern tradition of progress and the ongoing expansion of the boundaries of the invention is now dead. Originality is dead. In conclusion, Lassen claims that humans are stuck with a constant crisis of meaning, "a dark room from which we cannot escape".

A similarly depressing analysis is presented by Fernando Pessoa. In his book, The Book of Disquiet, he describes a morning walk through Lisbon's streets. He begins the walk by looking at the street "without prejudice" but ends it by carrying the full ascendant of culture"; I progress slowly, dead, my sight is no longer mine, it is no longer anything: it is only the sight of the human-animal without wanting to inherit the Greek culture, the Roman order, the Christian morality and all the other illusions that make up the culture in which I feel.

This is a description that precedes the time of postmodern thought. The whole culture is revealed as a collection of illusions whose adoption turns us into the dead walking, leaving no room for unique personal authenticity.

In answer to Lassen and Pessoa, it can be shown that postmodernism is not only not a dead end, but it points in the direction of a way out from the trap of culture. To find the origin, the life, one has to pull out the compass that will guide us towards primary, pre-cultural thought patterns. Personal autonomy can replace failing Greek, Roman, Christian, or other ideologies. Postmodernism does us a great service when it comes and unloads the burden of meaning that culture has imposed on us. The culture was made possible by observing nature from above. The detached view from the above creates a sense of superiority and alienation from the natural world.

Culture deprives us of the possibility of treating another human as a natural non-ideologic creature, creating interpersonal alienation. Postmodernism confers the ability of an outside look at the phenomenon of looking from the above. This ability allows us to locate the problematic aspects of looking from the above, one of the cornerstones of culture and progress. This view will enable us to reshape our lives without needing external meaning. This freedom allows us to accept every human being as a natural being while understanding and accepting the existence of cultural constructions as part of his identity.

Internalization of the postmodern reexamination technique is important for retirees. Work is one of the main pitches on which the ideological tournament is played. Without work, we are free to review the social field, this time devoid of the filter of cultural construction.

Primary vision, as unmediated as possible, leads to proper action. Students of Buddhism often ask: "How will I be motivated to do things if I shed the feelings of rejection and passion that result from classifying things as good and bad?" The answer is that the motivation will come for the right reasons, not out of desire but out of integration into the natural, flowing, and changing order of things. An act resulting from the right cause is done right. Being part of nature is not an ideological order; it is the natural order preceding the formation of ideologies. It was the secret of peace.

. . . .

Work is our Life, but ...

To summarize

- Work is the ultimate loss of autonomy and ownership of our time.

- Employing people for most of their lives requires suppression and surveillance measures.

- Making work a value in an ideological framework facilitates oppression.

- Specialization causes the limitation of thought.

- Work and the people who perform it have become commodities like all commodities.

- Work provides occupation and meaning - leaving it is scary and creates a void.

- Capitalism exploits workers to the limit of their physical and mental capacity through competition between companies and between workers.

- Stress kills - work shortens lives.

WHAT CAN WE DO?

- Recognize that many tensions are created by the system, not by our lack of physical and mental abilities.

- Explore the possibility of reducing the role work plays in your life.

> "When a man tells you that he got rich through hard work, ask him: 'Whose?"
>
> (Don Marquis)

Work is a punishment. At least, that's what the authors of the first chapters of Genesis thought. They describe Adam and Eve's deterioration from an idyllic life in paradise to a state of expulsion and punishment.

According to the bible authors, after the fateful deed of eating the apple of knowledge, God does not carry out the death penalty he threatened earlier. God imposes on humans another punishment, apparently close in severity to the death penalty. Humans are doomed to labor until the end of their days.

Since the writing of the Bible, much water has flowed in the ideological river. Work has turned from punishment to the most important and valuable element in our lives.

Work determines our self-perception, economic position, place of residence, nature of our vacations, and attire. It has an enormous impact on our mood, social status, and the state of our health.

From the age of four, as we go to kindergarten, we enter an education system that prepares us for the next twenty years to function in the world of labor.

Work allows most readers of this book to live a standard of living that is much higher than that of their grandparents. The job and the workplace define our identity. The question: "What do you do?" (meaning "what is your job") is usually the first question and often the only one that we ask a new acquaintance. Although few of us will admit it, work is more important to us than family. Suppose we are faced with completing an important presentation for tomorrow or playing with our children. It is clear what we will decide. Likely, we are unaware of the position that such a decision represents. Relocating to a faraway city or even a country for a career is increasingly common, despite the familial implications.

Work provides us with an intellectual interest and a challenge with which we prove our skills to ourselves and others. Alongside, it provides a simple enjoyment of the opportunity to express mental ability. Success at work is easily measurable, clearly rewarding in terms of money and status, and even more valued by society than success in less-defined areas like interpersonal relationships.

Indeed, many of those who succeed in work love it.

WORK AND GENETICS

Humans are not genetically adapted to work 12-8 hours daily for many consecutive months. Humans have never been pressured to withstand such a workload until the last two hundred years. Videos documenting the life of hunter-gatherer societies show us people who spend most of their time at rest, playing with their children, and talking to their family and friends. The anthropologist Richard Lee studied a hunter-gatherer society on the edge of the Kalahari Desert and measured the group's work hours for a month. He found that they 'work' an average of two hours a day (so far as hiking in nature and hunting activities can be considered work). Studies of hunter-gatherers' societies in other parts of the world have found up to five hours of engaging in 'work.'

I put 'work' in quotes because I remember the video about a group of natives from the Onga tribe in Little Andaman mentioned in the introduction. Three hunters wander in the blue coastal waters of a tropical island, a light spear in their hands. They talk to each other, occasionally throwing the spear into the water and taking it out with a fish fluttering on its head. After collecting some fish, they wrap them in broad leaves and bury them in the soft sand along with some hot stones to cook them. Richard Lee would measure about half an hour of 'work,' but most likely, the Onga would not understand what work he was talking about. To them, they were just fishing. With such an evolutionary background, no wonder fishing is a loved holiday activity.

How is the fishing of the Onga different from work?

Fishing is an activity with an immediate purpose. Work often involves producing a part of a product that most workers will not see completed and will never use. The Onga has independence in determining the time of activity, which takes place in the natural, open environment compared to the remote, closed work environment.

Work and mental and moral autonomy

The ultimate loss of personal autonomy occurs at work. We lose ownership of our time and often the freedom to act according to our basic moral values. Major scandals in pharmaceutical companies come to mind, but the pressure to twist moral values happens everywhere.

> *A Kibbuts' plastic sheet factory where I worked as a marketing manager suffered from stiff competition from importers. It became clear that the importers managed to survive despite the low-profit margins just because they cheated and marked a longer sheet length on the rollers.*
>
> *The way to win the competition was clear – indicating the sheet's weight and length. Weight, as opposed to a sheet length of several miles, can be easily measured for accuracy.*
>
> *The plan was met with hostility from our old-time sales manager. It turned out that we, the so-called credible producers, were also cheating.*

. . . .

Work as an ideology

The puritanical ethics of the work of the first settlers of North America are among the American cultural chromosomes today. Despite their technological advancement, Americans work more hours a day than anyone else.

Why has its ideological status changed from a punishment to a sacred value?

The history of labor is characterized by an increasing loss of personal autonomy.

The agricultural revolution initially robbed humans of the ownership of time, and the activity was dictated by the life cycle of the plants and animals they raised. However, they still controlled performing all the chores, and the proceeds were used only by them.

During the Industrial Revolution, the loss of autonomy peaked through the loss of ownership of time, resulting from the inability to perform tasks from beginning to end and the need for expensive machinery. This specialization in a limited part of the production process required establishing a hierarchical system to coordinate and organize the various stages of production.

Employing people for many hours in monotonous work under a hierarchical system required a marked increase in oppression. This unnatural situation was addressed by turning work into a first-rate cultural value so that workers would oppress themselves 'voluntarily' without feeling that their will was a consequence of social construction.

. . . .

In other words, the shift from looking at work from a natural activity to a source of difficulty and then to supreme value is a result of the change in the organizational structure of work from self-work to specialized work for an external organization.

The less the activity is compatible with primal human nature, the more explicit the ideological system must be to sustain it.

SPECIALIZATION AS A DUMBING PROCEDURE

Adam Smith, the great 19th-century English economist, provided the scientific basis for capitalism in his book The Wealth of Nations. He defined the miraculous 'invisible hand,' which optimizes the economy, allowing everyone to behave in a selfishly economic manner. This 'invisible hand' is supposed to result in an optimal allocation of resources for the benefit of all participants. And here in the Bible of capitalism, he writes: "the understandings of the greater part of men are necessarily formed by their ordinary employments. The man whose whole life is spent in performing a few simple operation.... generally becomes as stupid and ignorant as it is possible for a human creature to become."

Specialization is a general phenomenon, and the need for specialization stems from the need to control the vast accumulation of knowledge. Thus, a history professor is a history professor of medieval Rome. His understanding of other areas is relatively superficial. Teaching is a burden to him because the activity is repetitive, and its timing is imposed. Even professors, who apparently hold the pinnacle of intellectual freedom and autonomy as employees, end up in a little intellectual corner.

The same goes for doctors who once treated humans and now often only treat hearts or kidneys.

So it is among the intellectual elite, and so it is for most of us. Our world is limited to our field of work, a narrow practice area that contributes little to our intellectual development.

Work Makes Us a Product in the Market

Another value that is a result of recent cultural development is competition.

Turning labor into a commodity is exemplified by the frequent use of the term 'labor market.' Defining work as a market means competition between us. Unconsciously, we begin to treat ourselves as a product. Product development and improvement to suit market requirements are becoming our ultimate goals. In the process, we are moving further and further away from our authentic being.

Even if we do not always notice competition with colleagues, it does not mean it does not exist. Our co-workers are just as scared as we are of the possibility of losing their job.

But this is not the only competition we enter when we enter the gates of the modern world of work. Employers have learned that an involved worker is a loyal and hardworking worker. They will do anything to ensure that employees are emotionally invested in the competition the business is in with other companies in the market. With sophisticated psychological means, the capitalist transfer some of the concern for business risk to the employee. Thus, the employee competes with his fellow workers and is emotionally involved in his company's competition.

The fear of freedom

Given the industrial organization of our lives since we were children, it is no wonder that fear of freedom is one of the main phobias awaiting us in retirement. We have a hard time imagining a situation where we will be responsible for creating our daily schedule. We fear disintegration of ourselves without a framework that defines us and decides for us how to make our time meaningful.

The health hazards of work-stress

People get sick and even die from work. It is safe to say that work shortens most people's lives.

The basic process that causes the high risk is the body's response to emotional stress or - in other terms - anguish or distress.

A distinction must be made between challenge and stress. A challenge excites us physically and emotionally and encourages us to learn new things and develop new abilities. After meeting the challenge, we are satisfied and relaxed.

Stress occurs when the job requirements cannot be fulfilled because we are not qualified or the job requirements are impossible to meet. Relaxation becomes exhaustion, and satisfaction becomes stress. Work becomes an optimal infrastructure for developing an illness, injury, and diminished self-worth.

Stress is defined as a violation of emotional balance by a physical or psychological factor. The modern world produces ongoing background stress. In addition to frustration at work, national conflicts, social tensions, crime, high unemployment rates, aging, and family are all sources of stress.

In a N.I.O.S.H. study, 25% of workers said that stress at work is the top stressor, and 75% reported more stress at work today than in the past. The average absence due to anxiety, stress, and nerve problems is 25 days compared to 6 days for other reasons.

In addition to the pressure in the workplace, there is also external pressure. Frequent technological changes raise uncertainty regarding the future of jobs or the ability to keep up to date to meet job requirements.

This phenomenon causes individuals and businesses to run just so as not to lag behind their technologically up-to-date competitors. The increasing pace of competition due to frequent technological changes increases the perceived risk for the job. Studies suggest a strong link between job insecurity and low-level physical health overall.

Continuous competition causes constant emotional stress. The body's response to stressful situations is no different, whether it is an encounter with a lion or stress from not being invited to an important internal meeting.

Such stressful situations occur to us many times a day and sometimes continuously. Short episodes do not cause damage to the body. Still, an unresolved state of tension leaves the biological systems constantly activated.

Evidence of stress involvement at work in chronic cancers, cardiovascular disease, muscle and bone diseases, increased injuries, suicide, autoimmune disorders, and mental disorders such as depression are also beginning to accumulate.

To deal with stress at work, it is necessary to address all the factors - personal, interpersonal, and systemic.

What can each of us do to reduce the effect of stress?

The first thing to recognize is that the capitalist system exploits people the way it exploits machines, to the limit of their capacity. This recognition can reduce the feeling of guilt from our inability to complete all the tasks. We should also know that most of our co-workers are exposed to similar pressures, and we are not alone in being unable to meet workplace demands without high stress and frustration.

Identifying the sources of stress is important.

Stresses arising from a mismatch between personal skills and job requirements require the courage to change the workplace or the job. Some solutions are self-employment, consulting, or part-time employment. Over-promotion is a constant stress factor at work, no less than a lack of promotion. Here, neutralizing stress requires recognizing our limited ability and even giving up a coveted position. Such a step involves relinquishing the ego.

The ultimate solution with the optimal long-term impact is to stop working. Ask yourself a simple question: "Would I continue to come to work every day even if I did not receive financial compensation?" A negative answer to this question, provided that the pay from your work is not an existential necessity, indicates that the time has come to seriously consider retiring.

EMOTIONAL NUMBNESS

Another effect that work has is on our emotional state; it makes us emotionally numb. Competitiveness and the constant conflicts at work activate alienation mechanisms in us that leave no room or energy for emotions.

> *Only after I retired from work I returned to reading fiction. Until then, I could not bring myself to be a partner in the sufferings of others, even those purely literary. I lacked an emotional capacity and rarely watched drama films for the same reason. I preferred to shrink emotionally. I refrained from asking my psychotherapist wife about her work to not burden myself with additional emotional weight. It is clear to me that this emotional opacity was also*

....

felt in my relationship with family members. After
retiring, my curiosity and interest in stories with
an emotional aspect have increased.

We are so rooted in the world of discipline and work and believing in its necessity that we cannot comprehend its high price. To do this, we must adopt an external perspective, preferably from other periods. Only in this way can we understand the extremism of our current situation.

Another point to think about in the context of work as a central value in our lives is that work is becoming less and less moral. Work often means partnering in a global project to create products and services that most of us see as unsustainable at its current pace. The resources of our little sphere are running out. In addition, the planet is becoming polluted at a rate that begins to bring natural disasters to hundreds of millions of people and thousands of species of animals and plants. At the same time, we consume as if there is no tomorrow.

Anyone who retires reduces the pace of this project by something and thus makes a modest contribution to slowing down the deterioration of our ailing planet. Alongside the moral aspect of retirement from work is an opportunity for personal development that the retiree can only dream of while working.

SIMPLICITY - THE PURSUIT OF HARMONY WITH THE PRIMAL HUMAN

TO SUMMARIZE

- Simplicity has a refining aspect beyond financial savings. It has elegant elements.

- Simple people tend to be more attentive to the world's and others' needs.

- Fashion is a collaboration of manufacturers and marketers to force you to buy things you don't need.

- Simplicity reduces personal alienation and brings happiness.

WHAT CAN WE DO?

- Be aware of the influence of fashion on your life.

- Learn about simplifying life. It may pave your way to early retirement.

The concept of simplicity connects all the issues discussed so far - the primal human as a model, equality, autonomy, and ego.

The desire for simplicity can be seen as a mental answer that tries to correct the over-complexity of modern life, being a deviation from the initial, natural, simple lifestyle.

Many scientists have noticed the power of simplicity. They have determined that the simpler theory should be preferred when two ideas fit the same observations. St. Thomas Aquinas' claim that nature does not add an unnecessary complication is very intuitive. Similarly, Newton said that nature is pleased with simplicity, and Galileo said that nature does not multiply unnecessary things. It uses easy and simple means to create the effects and does nothing in vain. Modern physicists are looking for a unifying law to explain all physical phenomena, meaning maximum simplification of physics.

Simplicity and aspects of elegance and economy are both separate and intertwined. A Japanese Zen garden is a fascinating example of this. Gravel and rocks are carefully arranged in asymmetrical order. A wavy pattern in the gravel hints at the sea, and the stones are seen as islands. Thrift means elegance in the result.

A similar view can be found in Western art. Picasso said, "Art is the removal of the unnecessary."

Amos Oz, an Israeli writer, added a similar perspective on simplicity: "You can't teach people to write, but you can teach them to delete". Anyone who has written knows it takes talent and experience to identify the unnecessary and arrive at a more understandable and effective sentence, which is usually the simpler one.

The roots of the simplicity movement lie in a philosophical tradition thousands of years old. Many philosophers dealt with one aspect or another of simplicity. Still, the most prominent of them is Epicurus. Simplicity is at the center of his teachings and is a condition for him to attain happiness. He demonstrated the way to achieve happiness with the help of simplicity through his early retirement from work and his settlement with friends on the farm to live a simple and independent life. Next to him must be the Buddha, who preached to be content with what is necessary and not to cling to passions that are impossible or difficult to achieve. Similarly, Dr. Weston Price says about the Torres inhabitants, "needs that are not easily fulfilled simply do not exist".

Simplicity is a central principle in some sects of Christianity and other religions. Even secular people, in recent centuries, have praised simplicity as a miracle. Prominent among them is the American thinker Henry David Thoreau. He tried to live simple lives and wrote a popular book about it called Walden, which became a model for many young Americans.

The ideal of simplicity in Christianity has spawned several religious factions, such as the Puritans, the Quakers, the Amish, the Mennonites, and the Shakers.

Among the recent political leaders, Mahatma Gandhi stands out as an example of emphasizing simplicity as a way of life. He lived on a farm that provided all his needs and dressed as the last of the poor in India from a fabric he made himself.

THE SIMPLE LIFE MOVEMENT

'Simple Life' is now a substantial social movement. Its followers choose to live by it for many reasons, including quality time for family, children, and friends, health, stress relief, and thrift for its own sake. Others choose this way of life for political, ecological, and social reasons.

The followers of the simple life feel that it is impossible to buy with money our way to happiness in a deep sense of personal satisfaction.

Duane Elgin, one of the movement's leading thinkers, defines it as a simple way of life only on the outside but very rich on the inside. Elgin, who has been writing and lecturing for the past thirty years on simplicity, notices several tendencies that characterize people who have chosen a life of voluntary simplicity. They tend to:

- Invest their time and energy in spouses, children, and friends, volunteering to help others, and in civic activities to improve community life.

- Engage in the full development of their potential - the physical (running, cycling, walking), the emotional (developing skills of intimacy), the mental (self-study, external courses), and the spiritual (calmness and empathy for others).

- Feel an intimate connection to the earth and nature.

- Be more attentive and empathetic to the poor of the world, sensitive to social justice and equality in using the world's natural resources.

- Lower their personal consumption level. They buy fewer clothes, pay more attention to functionality, sustainability, and aesthetics, and less to fashion. They buy less jewelry, other decoration products, and cosmetics and spend vacations less commercially.

- Buy durable, easy-to-repair products that do not contaminate in their production or use.

- Change their diet from processed products to healthier and more natural products.

- Reduce confusion and complication in their private lives by selling or distributing rarely used objects, such as books, clothes, furniture, and appliances.

- Boycott unethical commercial companies.

- Recycle.

- Promote work that directly contributes to the world's well-being and enables a person to utilize his creative skills more efficiently.

....

- Develop abilities that contribute to self-reliance and reduced dependence.

- Prefer a more limited, humane work and living environment that promotes a sense of community, face-to-face contact, and mutual concern.

- Skew male and female roles in a non-gendered direction.

- Appreciate the simplicity of non-verbal communication - silence, hug, touch, look.

- Use holistic medicine that emphasizes disease prevention.

- Support goals like rainforest protection and saving endangered species and tend to use non-violent means in these efforts.

- Change the means of transportation they use in favor of public transportation, small and fuel-efficient cars, living close to the workplace, cycling, or walking.

Some economists try to adapt the science of economics to assumptions of simplicity and sustainability. Among the most prominent thinkers is James Robertson, who wrote a book called: 'A New Economy of Sustainable Development. Robertson argues that sustainability will require a thought revolution in economics from a paradigm of maximizing revenue to reducing spending. The principles that Robertson promotes are:

- Giving power to the individual (Empowerment) instead of the model of economic dependence that exists today.

- Systematic saving of resources and preservation of the environment.

- The transition from 'wealth of nations' (an economic concept of the 19th century) to the idea of one world.

- The transition from an international economy to an ecologically sustainable, decentralized economic system.

- Restoration of political and ethical factors to a central place in the economy and treatment of the problematic existence of business factors driven only by long-term profit.

- Respecting quality values at the expense of quantity values.

- Respect for feminine values (affection, giving), not only masculine values (power, competition).

Another thinker, David Wann, suggests that we ask ourselves three questions:

- What is the purpose of consumerism?

- What is economics for?

- Why are we not happier now than when we began the journey to wealth and abundance?

He replies that the simple way of life is the opposite of the modern desire for wealth and deals less with quantities and more with preserving cities, traditions, and nature.

Instead of emphasizing material wealth, he proposes to develop, in balance, the invisible abundance of experiential richness.

Simplicity is not asceticism. One can buy the most expensive product to achieve maximum reliability that will

. . . .

save preoccupation with product maintenance and still operate on the principle of simplicity.

Simplicity is not a sign of failure; simplicity can be a sign of smart choice. Precisely simplifying life can leave more room for life.

An attempt at simplicity creates a person's presence toward himself. Despite the dictates of advertisement and fashion, people do not act distracted and automatically, leaving room for their personality, self-presence, and unique presence to be expressed.

Simplicity does not mean boredom or stinginess. Given the boundless passion for objects we are subject to, simplicity can sometimes signify sanity. The primal human lived in simplicity, while we live in complexity. Can we simplify our lives and enjoy the process and the result?

A tremendous mechanism of advertising and social conventions works against us. We are so deeply immersed in consumerism that the very act of uncalculated, extravagant consumerism is used to signal to the environment - "I have!". A well-considered expenditure of money may be wrongly seen by others as a sign of money scarcity.

Dawn Elgin, speaking of voluntary simplicity, says that to live more according to will means to live more intentionally and purposefully - in short, to live more consciously. We cannot be intentional when we are distracted from life, and we cannot have a purpose when we are not present. Therefore, to act voluntarily is to be aware of ourselves as we progress through life. It means that we should pay attention to our

. . . .

actions in the outside world and ourselves when we act - to our inner world.

It is important to distinguish between striving for simplicity and stinginess. Stinginess borders on saving at the expense of the other. Giving a tip lower than usual for no reason is due to cheapness. The result is frugality, but it involves unfair behavior that deprives the waiter, most of whose modest income comes from an accepted practice of giving tips. Similarly, buying a cheap and low-quality item can come from stinginess, which, while not causing harm to the other, is equally blind. When we succeed in buying something cheap and good, it is not stinginess. It is the result of wisdom, effort, and awareness.

Meaning and Happiness

To summarize

- Death is the father of all anxieties. The way to deal with fears is by using logic. When we exist, death does not exist; when it exists, we do not exist.

- Time is a social construction like any other construction. It stems from our ability to take ourselves out of nature and examine it passing by. The culture uses the time to impose discipline, and surrendering to a schedule means losing autonomy.

- Meaning is the need for purpose. The quest for meaning is a relatively late phenomenon that stems from a feeling that we can and should influence the world. Bigger meanings allow for deeper satisfaction, but there is a danger of losing our personal moral bar to the morality of the gurus.

- The need for meaning is also related to the compulsive preoccupation with the past and future.

- Happiness is largely a result of interpreting reality.

. . . .

- Epicurus, the quintessential philosopher of retirement, upholds freedom, friendship, and philosophizing as the keys to a happy life.

- Modern research on happiness concludes that a life of continued wellbeing is commensurate with the primary human lifestyle

- Our limited ability to simulate makes us overestimate the impact of various factors or events on our happiness. We can return to a natural level of satisfaction even after disasters.

WHAT CAN WE DO?

- Fear of death - according to de Montaigne, the solution to fear of death is to deal with it every day, know it, and study it to get used to it until we are not afraid of it. The recognition of death frees us from all submission and limitation.

- Time - defeating the tyranny of time can be done through spontaneity and focusing on the present.

- Meaning - don't be a slave to the meanings of previous generations. You are not committed to their purposes if it does not make you happy.

- Acknowledge the absence of external meaning.

- Commitment creates meaning - the action makes the commitment.

- Look for meaning in opportunities to help others. We may have a genetic drive to help.

- Accept that we have no control over most events.

- Reality is a screen for projecting an interpretation - choose an interpretation for your life story that will serve your happiness.

Thoughts of meaning, happiness, and death accompany us throughout our lives, but they naturally occupy a growing place in retirement. The lack of need (or opportunity) to go to work every day completely changes the game's rules. It requires the retiree to re-examine and re-formulate his perceptions of happiness and meaning. Progress in age and the retirement stage being the last in the order of life: childhood - training - work - retirement also leads to more involvement in thinking about death.

MEANING

A story: Midnight. I lay awake in my bed. Unusually, I could not fall asleep. Even my wife's calm breaths made me feel uncomfortable. The knock on the door at this late hour did not surprise me for some reason. The pace of knocks was strange. It wasn't a pace intent on urgency or a desire for immediate attention. The knocks were calm and confident, slow and measured in intensity. The feeling of discomfort I felt over the last few hours intensified. Another force, not mine, overcame me and led me toward the door. A thin light aura familiar from Raphael's paintings penetrated the spaces between the door and the lintel. At once, it was clear to me who the visitor was. My first reaction was to go back to bed. I had no intention of cooperating. 'Back to the door,' came an authoritative and calm voice from the stairwell. I stopped.

'He sees me through the walls' A paralyzing thought went through my mind. I went to the door and opened it. There was no surprise here. The old man with a professional appearance was dressed in white and even had wings.

'How did they know that in the stories?' I thought. He hurried into the room and sat uninvited on the couch. 'that's it?' I asked. I had no desire to say much. 'Usually yes, usually I have to hurry,' he sighed. 'What do you mean 'usually? Is this time different? ' I asked in a tone that did not hide my hopes. 'It's up to you, but ...' he said. 'Then,' I told him at once, 'kindly continue to the others waiting for you.' He smiled faintly. It was clear to him that none of the others were really waiting for him.

'The story is not so simple,' he said. He thought for a moment and seemed to debate how to put it. 'Look,' he said, 'you are a special case that repeats itself once in one hundred and thirty thousand years. 'A special case?' I thought to myself, this already sounds less bad. I began to relax.

He continued, 'Once in one hundred and thirty thousand years, one apple falls from the tree of life, which still stands in the same corner of heaven. On the day the apple falls, we hold the "Thirteen Lottery "between those on the death quota of the day. The person who wins the lottery is granted an option", he raised his voice, "I emphasize, an option! To live extra one hundred and thirty thousand years until the next apple falls."

. . . .

'To live another 130,000 years?... I take it!!" I shouted to myself. I informed him that I was taking advantage of the option here and now.

'Wait,' he said with a bitter, all-knowing smile. 'Let me add to you that there is no regret option! Once you have decided, you must live throughout the period. And now let me tell you about the woman I'm going to after I'm done here. He ordered me to sit on the chair in front of him with a wave of his hand.

I was completely calm. I was peaceful at levels I had not known before. I had one hundred and thirty thousand years to hear all the stories in the world! I sat down.

'Her name sounds like 'oh' and 'hu.' She is, of course, the winner of the previous lottery; therefore, today is her turn to die. A few years after she chose the option, her husband and later her children died, and a few years later, her grandchildren were gone. Pretty soon She lost her enthusiasm for life. Things started to repeat themselves, and she, although living in a small and intimate group of her contemporaries, remained quite lonely. She always knew that if she developed emotional ties, they would last for only a few years, and then the inevitable separation would come. The recognition that it would be five thousand life cycles before her death did not encourage her, to say the least.

During the next thirty thousand years, her peers' shape and minds changed, and she was considered 'archaic.' Suddenly other, more intelligent human beings with more developed linguistic abilities appeared in the area. Although she did not fear them, for she knew that she could not get killed, she was not able to connect with them. After the last of her species disappeared, she wandered into a forest a thousand miles away. There she lived alone until about ten thousand years ago.

Later, the members of the new species, your species, the species you call the intelligent species, invented agriculture, and the forest area began to dwindle. She had to move her residence to increasingly remote places. Tonight, I will meet her in one of the valleys in the Himalayas. She has somehow managed to hide from the locals for thousands of years. They rarely see her footprints and even have given her a name, Yeti, but to this day, she has managed to avoid meeting them. '

He finished, got up, put his hand on my shoulder, and said in an empathetic but matter-of-fact tone: 'You must decide now. His hand did not move from my shoulders. The light in the living room turned off slowly. I felt my wife's soft palm on my shoulder. "Mikosh,' she whispered, 'you look like a dead man walking. Did you have a bad dream?"

Death means nothing to us

Many philosophers, poets, and writers write about death, and everyone who thinks deals with death. A basic difference between humans and animals is that we know that we will die one day.

Epicurus suggested using philosophy to treat the primary source of anxiety in our lives, death, with logic. In his letter to his friend Manukaus, he summarized his doctrine regarding

. . . .

death: "Get used to believing that death is nothing to us. When we exist, death is not; and when death exists, we are not. All sensation and consciousness end with death; therefore, there is neither pleasure nor pain in death. The fear of death arises from the belief that in death, there is awareness."

Once we have lost the fear of death, all other anxieties, according to Epicurus, are perceived as marginal and no longer interfere with attaining happiness. What can scare those not afraid of the end of life?

The inventor of the literary essay genre, Michel de Montaigne, a 16th-century Frenchman, writes of death: "Let us learn bravely to stand our ground and fight him and to begin to deprive him of the greatest advantage he has over us, let us take a way quite contrary to the common course. Let us disarm him of his novelty and strangeness, let us converse and be familiar with him, and have nothing so frequent in our thoughts as death. Upon all occasions represent him to our imagination in his every shape... Where death waits for us is uncertain; let us look for him everywhere. The premeditation of death is the premeditation of liberty; he who has learned to die has unlearned to serve. There is nothing evil in life for him who rightly comprehends that the privation of life is no evil: to know how to die delivers us from all subjection and constraint."

Again, an examination of the thinking of the primal human can teach us something about the pre-cultural relationships with death.

. . . .

The earliest burial was discovered in Israel on the southern edge of the Carmel and dates to 130,000 years ago. This means that until then, humans probably did not see the need to bury the dead. In the Hadza tribe, it was not customary until recently to bury the dead. They perceive death as part of the course of life. They do not need to commemorate the deceased by burial, although they respect their ancestors.

TO BE RELEASED FROM THE PRISON OF TIME

Our sense of life and death is inextricably linked to the sense of time. Strange as it may sound, time is not necessarily a real thing. It is hard to accept this for us, who live minute after minute with time. We cannot escape the presence of time. As difficult as it may be, I will try to convince you that time can be regarded as a cultural construct like any other.

A definition of time can be a flow from the past through the present to the future. But the past does not exist in reality; it existed in the past, and so is the future, which will exist only in the future.

The present is also something between the past and future that we define as the present. We live in a certain year, a certain month, a certain day, a certain minute, a certain second, and so on. Is the present the year? The hour? the second? It's all a matter of a definition we choose to use at the time, not of real physical reality.

Every second that comes to our consciousness (a process that takes time) has already passed, and it belongs to a past we have agreed does not exist as time.

We do not actually have a clear objective sense of time. Time passes faster and even disappears when we are involved in a subject that occupies us in every vein of our soul. We would expect that time that passes quickly will not reach the stage where it is gone.

But time is something whose presence is felt precisely when it is slow or hardly moves when we are bored. In the story Mr. Lublin's Shop, Shay Agnon writes: "Twisting and stubborn is the time. They want to expand it, it shortens, they want to shorten it, and it lengthens."

The metaphor of flow is inevitable when talking about time, but does flow describe time? Calculating each current requires using time units. Water flow, for example, is measured in units of cubic meters per hour. But how do we measure time if time is a current, and we need time to measure a current?

Science also denies the existence of time.

"The whole consciousness is a consciousness of time", wrote the American poet Dennis Levertov. A sense of time is needed to see the world from the outside, to be aware of the world. We adopt an external point of view, and the world passes before us. This is the sense of time, without defining it to ourselves as such consciously. In ancient times, when we were so immersed in nature, we arguably did not have a strong sense of time. The more technology removes us from nature, the more our sense of time intensifies. The saying "time is money" was also true in the days of the Egyptians and Assyrians 5000 years ago. Still, it was practiced and assimilated as a common saying only in the nineteenth century, the industrial age, when our awareness of the passing of time increased.

As productivity increases, the economic value of time increases in absolute terms. With it, the sense of time is strengthened. Books are written, and electronic diary systems are developed to efficiently use time. With the advancement of technology, all our activities have entered a scheduled regime. Industrialization of production requires everything to be registered and predetermined: set-up time, start time, meeting time, time back home, TV news time, and so on. Many minutes of the 1,440 minutes in the day are scheduled.

In a pre-planned activity, in most cases, someone else sets a schedule (work hours, TV schedule). No wonder the first commandment taught children in school is not to be late, and the army sanctifies adherence to deadlines. The need to sanction respect for time shows that it is unnatural.

In psychology, one of the obvious symptoms of a clinical obsession is an abnormal preoccupation with the subject of time. Time "is the enemy of eros and deep ally of the order of repression", John Zerzan writes in a long article on 'Time and its Discontents.'

Is it possible to escape completely, even for a short time, from the prison of time to a state of timelessness? Meditation in a Buddhist format tries to bring us into such a state. The state of emptiness sought is the emptiness of rejection or passion, including denial and desire for the past, present, and future. A meditator who reaches nirvana, the void of thought, is freed from the yoke of time but few can or are willing to devote the time and effort to reach this state.

If not canceled, how can one still dim the oppressive touch of time?

If time is indeed cultural construction, it can be controlled to some extent through thinking. Active and spontaneous involvement in nature distances us from the external view of nature. It thus weakens, to some extent, the sense of time.

The phrase "Eat, drink and be merry for tomorrow we die" builds the walls of time around us even more. This saying should be replaced by the motto "Today and Spontaneous". There is nothing wrong with enjoying anything legal and moral. There is nothing wrong with spontaneously wanting to do it today, not because we will die tomorrow but because spontaneous action somewhat eliminates the burden of time.

Doing so today, unplanned, will reduce the place of yesterday and tomorrow. Thus spontaneity, albeit temporarily, breaks through the prison walls of time, and surprise breaks time. Spontaneity is the substrate on which surprise grows.

BETWEEN TIME AND MEANING

A poem:

Sigmund Wolf,
My father's father's father,

. . . .

My Great Grand
was ...
the truth is
I have no idea who he was.
I found his name,
Dwindling
On a branch of ink,
Black dry leaf,
In the family tree diagram.
I hope he did not live for me,
Of a generation that he did not know.
I hope he dried up slowly,
for his sake.
Whether he did or did not,
His foreignness inspires me with peace.
His oblivion is my oblivion.

Did Sigmund Wolf, my great-grandfather, have any meaning in his life? Did this citizen of the Austro-Hungarian Empire have typical Austro-Hungarian ideals? Imperial meaning? Religious meaning? As the poem says, I have no idea. And since I have no idea, I guess future generations, who will be added to the same family tree, will have no idea who I was. This thought makes me happy. It frees me from the need to live my life for the sake of future generations. To give birth, grow, help, and support, yes. To live (or die) for the sake of future generations - no and no.

Taking a little air out of the words 'meaning' and 'happiness,' we will start as usual with deconstruction,

'There is no happiness without meaning' is another one of those assumptions we haphazardly accept.

Our world is divided into people who have found meaning and those who seek meaning. Could it be that there are today, or were there ever happy people who did not see and did not even seek meaning?

These can be, to most of us, only bums. At this point in the book, there is no longer any need to guess: it is quite clear that early humans did not look for meaning. For millions of years, people on Earth did not know they had to look for meaning. Did not know there was meaning, and yet they were happy. Those hunter-gatherers remain content, as anthropologists and researchers who have met them attest. They were more satisfied than most people who had instilled in them the need to seek meaning from the day they were born.

The quest for meaning may be a by-product of the feeling of omnipotence, which came to us with the process of taking over nature. A desire for meaning can easily be interpreted as a human's attempt to embrace the divine ability to have a good influence on the planet.

THE GREAT EXTERNAL MEANING

One of the proofs of the need for meaning as a complementary part of our sense of omnipotence is that the higher the meaning, the more universal and valued it is. Sources of great meanings such as socialism, religion, and nationalism assure us that if we fulfill our role with dedication, we will have a meaningful life. The higher the personal sacrifice required, the higher its reward in meaning. The sense of satisfaction stems from belonging to a great and important entity. Fulfilling the commandments assures us a sense of security and control over our lives.

From the description of Captain Cook's visit to the Easter Islands, which appears in the chapter on the ego, one can also learn about this subject. Placing the huge sculptures on a family stage was an expression of the power of the family. It must have given great meaning to the family members engaged in the craft. They were dealing with something far more important than their small, personal, simple story. When we draw meaning from a big story, an ideology like religion or nationality, we tend to leave moralistic considerations in the hands of ancestors or leaders. Cutting down the last tree on Easter Island was apparently perceived as sacred even though, to any reasonable person, it was clearly suicidal.

By joining a goal greater than ourselves, we earn meaning with less effort. The problem is that if we are not vigilant, we may lose a sense of personal responsibility for actions done in the name of the same ideology and their consequences. This phenomenon of the abolition of personal responsibility in favor of meaning is a possible explanation for the atrocities frequently committed in the name of a religion, tribe, or state.

Our belief in a greater supreme meaning than ours is basically just faith. It cannot be otherwise against the background of our solid knowledge that we will all die sooner or later. A great external goal, lasting beyond death, is tempting and requires faith. It is clear to us that we will not be here to know if the plan has been effective and achieved the imagined target.

Such a belief requires a lengthy process of socialization, which our early ancestors most probably did not experience. Faith obliges us not only to give up today to receive tomorrow but to give up today so that someone else will receive after we die.

The absence of external meaning is a side effect of the fact that we will all die. The lack of external purpose can be seen as the lifebuoy thrown at us from the cruise ship to death. If we die, and everyone who comes after us will also die, any meaning can be but temporary and contemporary. It follows that aiming at a present-rich type of meaning, like that of a hunter-gatherer, could be a successful prescription for achieving happiness.

This recognition leads to wondering about the meaning of our existence as a species. For example, knowing the finality of cosmological bodies like the sun tells us that even the existence of humans is temporary. The human species is just one of the millions of species on one of the planets orbiting about a hundred billion suns in our galaxy, which is just one of a hundred billion galaxies in the universe. So, let's look at things in proportion - the existence of one temporary species on one planet in one solar system, in one galaxy out of a hundred billion galaxies, probably does not worry anyone except ourselves. We can't even claim to be useful to the existence of nature. After all, we are responsible for exterminating hundreds of thousands of other species.

. . . .

Millions of other species appeared and disappeared, including those very similar to us, like the Neanderthals.

Recognizing the lack of external meaning should make us boundlessly happy. It frees us from dragging heavy and unnecessary cargo throughout life. The enslavement of life to a noble cause that someone else has established requires relinquishing much of our autonomy and self-judgment.

The ability to come to terms with the fact that no external meaning casts causality into our lives frees us from the need to carry a heavy burden of a system of commandments and beliefs. It directs our power and energy to do things more relevant and important to our development as human beings. Deeds will be done out of altruism, but they will be done of our free will and not following a higher commandment.

We will be good to ourselves if we accept that life is a game, not an exercise. In the exercise, there is a solution (supreme meaning), and all we have left is to find the answer. In the game, we must draw new conclusions, be creative at every step according to the developments, and change planned moves. Even then, there is no guarantee that we will reach the goal or discover some purpose. On the contrary, the exercise has an endpoint, where we know we have arrived, but the game continues if we can and want it.

So much for the great significance of the Grand Histoire - the great story, which according to postmodernism, died a natural death. Some mourn its end, and others celebrate its disappearance.

SMALL PERSONAL MEANING

Our need for meaning is closely associated with our compulsive preoccupation with the past and the future.

Except for occasional references to ancestors, few primal humans deal with the past. The inauguration ceremony of the Onga youths in Little Andaman does not have a fixed date. Its date is set spontaneously, with a few minutes' notice. The spontaneity is not because they cannot be future-oriented but because it is not necessary most of the time.

If the future has meaning, then past events were not coincidences. There must be a story that connects past events and their link, by way of development, to the future. It is actually 'history,' a word that means 'story' in Latin.

One can summarize then that the need for meaning is especially strong in people who have leisure for worries about the future and a preoccupation with the past.

The retiree very easily enters this definition. He has leisure, a rich past, and worries about the future. When we worked, we did not have much time to think about the meaning of our lives, and our work gave us a considerable amount of meaning. Now the increased leisure allows us to plan the unfamiliar retirement space while raising awareness of the inevitable end in the future.

CREATING MEANING

Meaning and commitment are two concepts that have a strong interdependence. Meaning creates commitment, but there is an opposite direction - commitment makes meaning. Here is the key to finding meaning in those who seek it. Find something you are willing to commit to, realize this commitment through perseverance in the act, and the sense of meaning will grow spontaneously.

For example, the degree of meaning we feel during work is directly related to the level of commitment we develop toward the workplace. Unlike in the period of work, in the period of retirement, there is no need for totality.

A commitment that lasts for a while is enough for meaning to grow spontaneously. Repentant people advise us first to do, and then the belief will arrive. The act precedes the meaning, and doing the action creates an involvement that yields meaning.

The retiree, who is not bound by an externally dictated meaning, must determine the essence of the meaning. Will it be personal, national, universal, big, or small?

Following the primal human, it may be that the best chance to find meaning is in helping others. It makes sense that groups with people who tended to help others had a survival advantage over groups with more egoistic members. Thus, the siblings of the members of the successful groups, us, should also have a tendency to help. The extensive volunteerism among retirees supports this thesis.

HAPPINESS

Before we discuss the small, personal meaning, here are a few introductory words about happiness. Happiness, in the classical sense of the word, is a state that cannot exist for a long time. The pursuit of happiness is a childish aspiration. Many children's stories end with the sentence, "they lived happily ever after". It could very well be that if we did find the path to this kind of happiness forever, we would look like zombies. This simple definition of happiness means a state of supreme good feeling - euphoria, a short-term and rare state of mind.

A more plausible definition of purpose in life was introduced by the Buddha and Epicurus, although they used different terminology. Both interpreted happiness as a lack of suffering. At first glance, a definition of positive emotion as happiness through negation evokes resistance. Both define a situation in which we have no unfulfilled desires left. Is it possible to think of much greater happiness than this? But the state of happiness is achieved through the toil of restraint and taking the right steps.

Freud was even more humble than Buddha and Epicurus. Freud defined the purpose of psychology as the change of misery into common suffering. For him, happiness is an illusion, and a desire for happiness only leads to further frustration and despair, yet humans cannot give it up.

We may have to be content with something between the Buddha's consciousness-laden nirvana and Freud's melancholy. Perhaps the latter helps us feel the contrast between periods of satisfaction and suffering and happiness.

THE ONLY ORGAN OVER WHICH WE HAVE CONTROL

Reaching a state of happiness of the kind that Buddha and Epicurus speak of has to take place through the control of the mind.

A prerequisite for embarking on the path to happiness is to accept that most events in our lives are beyond our control. We have no problem accepting that the weather is out of our control. Still, for some reason, we expect to be in control of what happens to us. The reality is that our level of control is very far from what we would like to have.

In most cases, the very attempt to control the fate of those close to us causes them suffering and distances them from us. Giving up trying to control the lives of our spouses, children, parents, and friends may be the greatest good we can do for them and ourselves.

The need for control should be diverted to controlling our thoughts. Relaxation from the illusion of control over the reality around us diverts psychic energies to achievable goals. A change of attitude should not lead to a lack of interest and support for those around us. Still, we have to relinquish the drive to control their fate.

Fernando Pessoa's statement, "that episode of the dream we call reality", emphasizes our being the ones who define reality. We do it by classifying the real and the unreal. In the same way, we categorize reality into bad and good based mainly on cultural dictates. Hence, the conclusion is that we must strive for control over these cultural constructions.

Hunter-gatherers don't bother to control the lives of others. Anthropologists report the lack of need for control is also reflected in their children's education (or rather, in rearing). They place great trust in the desires and abilities of their children. This approach of trust leads to a process of personal growth, with which the word education has nothing to do with the industrial sense we have instilled. Education, as it is carried out with us, means control. For them, education is relaxation.

INTERPRETATION AND HAPPINESS

We produce reality in our thoughts.

Postmodernism formulates the phenomenon as providing interpretation. The non-identical perception of reality in different people eminent from different interpretations of the same facts. None of the interpretations are free of biases, which are the result of other cultural constructions.

If so, it can be said in postmodern language that the secret to a happy life is to choose an interpretation that will serve us best. The ability to select an interpretation requires a sober view of the burden of cultural constructions that each of us carries with it and an acknowledgment that our interpretation is not true or eternal. It is simply the one that happened to result at this time.

Recognizing the fallacies of ideologies frees us to adopt a system of interpretations appropriate to maximize our happiness at a given time.

. . . .

Psychological treatment is basically a process of changing interpretation. The patients tell the therapist their stories. The story is never free of interpretation, never a collection of cold facts. In most cases, the patient unknowingly omits important chapters in the story because they do not fit a current interpretation. Therefore, an important role of the therapist is to locate spaces in the narrative sequence and try to understand the reason for their disappearance. In a long, complex process full of objections and a search for a way, the therapist and the patient try to build an alternative interpretation that will minimize or eliminate the confusion and emotional suffering. Is the interpretation, the result of the treatment, more real? It does not matter as long as it is solid and appropriate for the patient at this stage.

Having dismantled the concept of happiness, let's discuss the path to happiness. The road to happiness assumes a way to go until we reach it at the end of the road. And what about the road? Maybe the way is a better target for happiness seeking? Indeed, even personal change, a change of perception, is a process that can bring happiness as we do it. What prevents us from experiencing happiness in the process of seeking happiness? The fear of change, of course. Epicurus talks about the way and the fear.

EPICURUS

Epicurus is the ultimate philosopher on the issue of retirement Paleo style. He retired from his post as a teacher early and established a commune farm near Athens where he and his followers could live in maximum simplicity.

Apart from being a genius on every scale, he was one of the most popular philosophers in the Hellenistic-Roman world for about 500 years after his death. Christianity then used its rising power to try to exterminate his memory. It has been successful for some time, but Epicurus' writings regained popularity a few hundred years ago and are still popular today. His fans included Spinoza, Pushkin, Schilling, and Jefferson. The farm communities that followed his teachings could still be found in the Hellenistic-Roman world for centuries after his death.

Epicurus was the only philosopher of his time in Greece to include women and even slaves among his disciples.

Much misunderstanding accompanies the teachings of Epicurus throughout the ages. Epicurus is considered wrongly by many to be the philosopher of hedonism. He set pleasure as the goal for a happy life. In contrast, philosophers of his time, including Aristotle, Plato, and the Stoics, put an ideal, timeless list of virtues as the goal.

Nature shows that all animals are attracted to pleasure and escape pain. Therefore, he believed this should also be the prescription for human happiness.

The use of the word 'pleasure' was the main source of attacks against him. To this day, the term Epicureanism is in English a synonym for a person who knows how to appreciate a good meal and a good wine. But the word pleasure was defined by Epicurus as the absence of pain. The greatest pleasure is when a person does not feel pain from any source, physical or emotional. The word pain appears in Epicurus more in the sense of suffering. And here, if the meanings are placed correctly, one can formulate the definition of Epicurus to the ideal state: a state of lack of suffering. If this sounds familiar, it is not a coincidence. The Buddha formulated an identical prescription for happiness two hundred years before him. The practice of the Buddha is certainly not hedonistic, but the idea is the same: the absence of suffering. Epicurus called the state of tranquility a state of calmness. Indeed, the outward appearance of a happy person, or rather satisfied or full of contentment, is usually an appearance of calm.

Contrary to his hedonic image, Epicurus took pains to explicitly limit his intention to the concept of 'pleasure.' He stated that it is better to give up short-term pleasure to ensure long-term pleasure. He preached simple eating and avoiding adultery. That is, he places the emphasis not on momentary pleasure but on lasting satisfaction and relaxation.

Following Epicurus, several modern philosophers interpret the ideal situation as a state without serious problems. For example, Epicurus recommends that we adopt a lifestyle that will provide us with food that can be easily obtained. We should not yearn for richer or more varied food or food that will make us uncomfortable later or food that is difficult to obtain. The result is that we are easily supplied with simple food. Thus, we can focus on other things without being distracted by trying to get special food.

Another option offered is to interpret calmness as a habit. Because simple food consumption is a habit, its acquisition does not require substantial mental effort and is not a source of suffering. Consumption of simple food becomes a habit, just as walking is a habit that does not need to be considered in detail when performed.

The recommendation to bring about behavioral changes to the level of a habit fits nicely with recent studies on behavior change. It was found that humans have a limited amount of avoidance ability per day. Suppose in the process of behavior change, we avoid many things in the morning. Then, avoiding temptations in the evening will be more difficult. But there is a point where avoidance becomes a habit and no longer involves effort. Anyone who has stopped smoking knows that the first few days are the hardest. If we persist, non-smoking will eventually become a habit.

Unlike Plato, Epicurus was against social reforms on a large scale. He preached a life of anonymity, far removed from public life. He didn't trust the crowd. He advised freeing ourselves from the prison of general education and politics - a phrase reminiscent of the distrust with which postmodern thinkers treat ideology of all kinds.

This approach of Epicurus stemmed from his general approach to philosophy. Epicurus did not deny the arbitrariness and randomness in life as clerics, and other philosophers tried. He accepted it as fate that originated from the atoms' motion coincidence. For him, the greatest damage is caused by living in the illusion that there is a divine direction for daily events.

The differences in attitude between Epicurus and other Greek philosophers can be seen as a reflection of the degree of trust in humans that the various philosophers, religions, and ideologies have. The detail in which Plato and his successors defined virtues reflects an assumption that humans will not behave properly without following their instructions. In contrast, philosophers like Epicurus and Buddha place their trust in humans. They talk to one degree or another about the conditions that will set a person free to live properly. How do we know what is right? The existentialist Simone de Beauvoir said that lacking a god to guarantee morality, it is up to the individual to create a bond with others through ethical action. The person is responsible for his world, which is not the work of supreme power but his own, where his failures are recorded with his victories. His job is to make the world significant and important "He alone can feel his success or failure."

Meticulous adherence to any ideology reflects a high level of anxiety. The thought that people will live without detailed guidelines about good and evil causes the listers of virtues to tremble. But it turns out that when you leave people to do what is right in their eyes, they normally do the right thing. There is no report that in Buddhist countries, the level of crime is higher, and there is no report on the involvement of Epicureans in acts of lawlessness. No postmodern thinkers have become murderers despite their disrespect for ideologies. In retrospect, it has been the proponents of a detailed list of "rights and wrongs" like fascists, communists, and religious extremists that brought most of the suffering to other humans.

This is one of Epicurus's main pieces of advice, which the retiree can apply: "Free yourself from the prison of general education and politics". Goals we did not choose, an ideology imprinted on us by public education, interfere with us being ourselves, interferes with us being. We must examine everything by logic, free from prejudice, says Epicurus. Logic is the best tool nature has given us to choose our way of life.

Epicurus proposed to place three milestones on the path to happiness, the three F's: Freedom, Friendship, and Philosophizing.

FREEDOM

Freedom is necessary to think logically and independently and to be able to perform what we decide to do. Freedom is the liberation from external factors such as the "prison of general education and politics" and internal slavery for hard-to-achieve desires. Since the days of the agricultural revolution, the most difficult freedom to achieve is economic freedom. Financial freedom can be achieved not only by accumulating wealth but also by reducing desires. Interestingly, the Epicurean concept of 'freedom' is identical to personal autonomy, a central component in the hunter-gatherer's life.

FRIENDSHIP

Friendship is a very central theme in Epicurus' teachings. He writes: "Of the things that wisdom provides for the whole life of the blessed human, the most important, by far, is friendship ... It is worth choosing any friendship because of the friendship itself even though the beginning of all friendship is in the good that it affects us". For Epicurus, the existence of friendships is part of the good life. Although companionship has the practical aspect of providing mutual security, it also has value for its own sake.

One can find the source for the sense of the vitality of friendships in the small primal group of family and friends. When Epicurus and his friends established a commune near Athens, working together to grow their food and discuss philosophy, they unknowingly returned to the community structure of a group of hunter-gatherers.

An example of our enormous need for friendship is given by anthropologist Kim Hill of the University of Arizona. Hill studied the Hiwi tribe living in the savannah on the border between Venezuela and Colombia. He reports that they walk up to sixty miles to visit friends.

In one of the Harvard group's studies that investigated positive psychology, they looked for the difference between very happy people and ordinary people. It turned out that very happy people are not distinguished by being religious, rich, or in a better physical condition. Nor do they look better and have no more good events or fewer bad events in personal history than others. The only variable that set them apart from their less happy brethren was that they were very friendly. They never spent time alone. Each of them was in a romantic relationship and had a wide variety of friends.

PHILOSOPHIZING

We have already emphasized Epicurus' doctrine regarding the importance of applying logic before action and overcoming anxieties such as the fear of death. Still, philosophizing was also a supreme source of pleasure for Epicurus. He wrote about three hundred books, but a considerable part of his and his friends' thinking was conducted jointly. Thus, the joy of friendship was associated with the pleasure of philosophizing.

Thinking in the sense of inquiry leads to knowledge, which has a great feature - it can be shared without losing a shred of it. On the contrary, if we share knowledge with a friend, he will likely add another aspect or information. Thus, the very distribution of knowledge will lead to its enrichment. One can also understand thinking more broadly - any primarily cerebral activity. This form also includes music, language, learning, and even games. Every activity that challenges the brain has the potential to bring happiness.

Besides the pleasure during the thought process, the ongoing practice of thinking has another long-term and very important effect - thinking and exploring make us interesting. Interesting to ourselves and interesting to others. Philosophizing not only makes us interesting, but it also builds us. "I think therefore I am", de Carte said, and we can expand and say that the richer we are in diverse thoughts, the more we exist. We exist more for ourselves, feel more alert, and live more.

The ability to be interesting is also closely related to the component of friendship in Epicurus' teaching. An important element in a good friendship, including marriage, is the ability to remain interesting and innovative. Boredom has been found in studies as a cause of divorce. At the beginning of the relationship, we try to captivate our partner. Still, after marriage, some tend to take their partners for granted. They are already ours, and the effort to impress can be put in a drawer. The result is a feeling, often mutual, of boredom and emptiness.

In this sense, the retiree is also in danger but can easily escape it. His partnership is usually many years old, so the potential for boredom is great. However, his time is in his hands to make himself more interesting and ensure that their spouse will act the same way.

In conclusion, the teachings of Epicurus are a gold mine for the retiree. The essence of his perception is retirement oriented. According to Epicurus, every unnecessary work moment is sinful for those for whom work is a source of suffering.

Happiness and our limited ability to produce a simulation

A Harvard researcher, Dan Gilbert, is researching the accuracy of our simulation capability. A person can imagine a complex hypothetical situation and determine whether it will cause him suffering or happiness. And here, Gilbert found that this system was naturally biased.

. . . .

Gilbert argues that we tend to exaggerate, both in evaluating the good results of positive events and the bad consequences of negative events. In the negative cases, the assessment is biased because it does not consider another capacity of our brain, which Gilbert defines as the ability to synthesize (produce) happiness. Therefore people who won the first prize in the lottery and those who suffered from paralysis return after about a year to the same happiness level they had before the event. The phenomenon is repeated in many situations - in college exam results, promotion or non-promotion at work, losses in sports, insults, and interpersonal infidelities. In all cases, the expectation is for a more significant change, for better or worse, in the level of happiness than what happens. Therefore, in his opinion, there is no room for exaggeration in efforts to achieve success or avoid failures. For example, stealing or lying are not worth the negative consequences of such steps. Both for a moral reason and because the result obtained will be less significant to our happiness than we expected.

A large part of the insurance industry seems to exist because we tend to portray the consequences of adverse events as more significant than they will be. We insure everything that moves and also everything that stands fixed. We insure property, the loss of which would not cause any change in our level of happiness. It may be that the whole phenomenon of pathological anxiety is a disruption of the simulation mechanism in the direction of exaggerating the negative consequences of events.

For almost two million years, we had to simulate relatively simple things according to the simple life of the hunter-gatherer. Today, we must deal with simulations that include many factors, most of which are abstract on a level that the primal human did not know.

A study on happiness in many countries shows that personal satisfaction is high at 18-24, begins to decline, and reaches a low among people aged 35-44. It rises again at 56-64 when it reaches a similar high for those aged 18-24. It seems, then, that time is working in our favor.

Boredom and Interest

To summarize

- Boredom cannot be the result of a lack of potential interest because the world is full of interesting things that are more accessible today than ever. The problem is with the barriers and inhibitions in ourselves.

- Boredom stems from the industrial revolution when our addiction to constant stimulation began.

- Boredom brings us closer to ourselves and shows us how empty our 'self' is without resonance and external support.

- Freedom leads us to the right and duty to fill our lives with contentment.

- Many more areas may interest us than we dare to imagine.

- Learning is an activity that eliminates boredom and makes us more interesting.

WHAT CAN WE DO?

- Welcome boredom, as a transitional stage between slavery and freedom, as a time for self-study.

- Try different fields. The price of making a mistake isn't high.

- Research yourself, research other topics, and summarize your research in writing. Give expression to the desire for knowledge.

- Learn. Teach.

Retirees, free from parenting and working full-time, look forward to a life full of enjoyment. Less stress, more time for the spouse, travel, children, grandchildren, hobbies, rest, and spirituality are our expectations. But on the side of expectations lurks the fear of boredom.

There is nothing more frightening to the potential retiree than boredom. The potential retiree and not the actual retiree because here, too, the simulation mechanism described in the previous chapter works to create incorrect expectations.

The deep fear of leaving work as a way of life stems partly from losing the cohesive sense of identity that has been nurtured for years. Still, a significant amount of the fear also has to do with fear of boredom, fear of meeting the void.

There is no reason to be bored nowadays; most educated retirees do not complain about boredom. Anyone who has done mentally challenging tasks in their working life can now easily find similar challenges even during retirement.

It is not uncommon to find people aged 50 to 90 in the lecture halls and cafeterias of various universities.

Let's try to break down the concept of 'boredom' into factors to befit the orderly doctrine of this book.

The Danish philosopher Kierkegaard defined life as an escape from boredom. Kierkegaard's approach is somewhat ironic but may have one or two principles we should consider. Kierkegaard's solution is to do everything upside down. He suggests going against all bourgeois principles like pleasure, friendship, and marriage. For him, friendship initially allows for mutual help. Still, after a short time, we find ourselves trapped in someone else's expectations. Marriage is a private case of friendship, where the spouses fixate on us in their perception. We become bored by the very fact that we are expected.

There is short-term boredom like the one that awaits you while waiting for a train or a flight. We will not deal with this type of boredom here but with the anxiety of long-term boredom, which is relevant for those considering retiring from work.

Long-term boredom cannot result from a lack of things to do or show interest in but from inhibitions that prevent the ability to join. The world is big and wide, and the possibilities are as open as ever. The problem is the fear that nothing will be interesting enough to excite us for many hours of the day.

The word 'boredom' appeared in English only in the 19th century. Was there no boredom before? Adam sits in his hut in Little Andaman with his friends and children and does nothing for hours. He does not have a TV, but he does not look bothered. On the contrary, he seems happy. It's just that boredom, like anything, is a relative matter. The word appeared when it appeared probably in the wake of the industrial revolution. The Western world is run by the rhythm of machines and computers. In the process, the rhythm and intensity of the stimuli have shifted from walking pace to chariot pace and from there to steam-powered machines, jet engines, radio waves, and digital data transfer. Periods of inaction have turned from a common situation to a state of failure in the high-tech era.

Boredom is a state of complete mental autonomy. No external factor dictates or encourages thinking in any direction. Work-life is a life in which the activity, at least eight hours a day, is determined for you by someone else. Stress at work accustoms us to a high level of stimulation. At work, we are usually in a state of heightened alertness whether the work interests us or even if we are on the verge of failure. In addition, we are exposed to about three thousand commercial messages a day and the abundance of media stimuli that surround them. We are addicted to this heightened state of alertness. We become adrenaline junkies. The process of retiring from work involves detoxification, like what every drug addict must go through.

We have already discussed the harms of emotional stress in the chapter on work. There is no reason to drag this pace of life into retirement, but what about the feeling of alertness? Won't we live like zombies after we no longer must work?

. . . .

Boredom is associated in our minds with anxiety. The phrase 'boring to death' demonstrates the terror of boredom. Boredom is a glimpse into the reality that awaits us after death. We fight boredom by trying to 'kill time.' A battle takes place between us and time. Boredom brings us together with ourselves, devoid of any external aids. There is a feeling that culture has abandoned us. We stay with ourselves; after a while, we have nothing to say to ourselves, and there is nothing to speak to us. The 'I' is empty, and the discourse is empty. The situation is a simulation of death. Interestingly, it is precisely this sense of lack of self that is the desire of the Buddhists. On the other hand, it confirms the postmodern claim that the 'I' is a construct and Winnicott's claim that the 'I' is the reflection of the other.

People who give up retirement for fear of boredom give up autonomy. Autonomy scares. They are anxious that they will not be able to fill life with contentment. They prefer a state of slavery to freedom. There is a saying, "an enslaved person waits for others to release him". Here we have a slave who does not want to be released because he does not know what to do with freedom. Is there a greater surrender than that? Is there greater proof than that of the damage caused to our free psyche by the industrial revolution? We have lost all self-will. We have lost our confidence in our ability to be ourselves. Sean Healy, the Irish philosopher, says boredom is the silent whip of modern culture. For many, it is the walls they build for the prison of their lives, the border beyond which they dare not cross.

Is boredom really that terrible? Maybe a period of boredom is part of the change process that a person has to go through when he goes from labor to freedom?

Boredom can be a time of relaxation, contemplation, and disconnection from the commercial world's takeover of the commercials and objects of our lives. What is Vipassana meditation, the Indian method of self-observation while avoiding speech and other stimuli, sometimes for several days, if not healing through boredom?

On boredom during meditation speaks a former English physicist named Bram, who now serves as head of a Buddhist monastery in Perth, Australia. He suggests taking the boredom and exploring it meditatively. Ask yourself what it stems from, what happens in the brain in a state of boredom, when we are bored and when we are not. The solution is particularly good because it gives us a key to a more general solution than Bram intended. His proposal also has a direction for solving the problem of long-term boredom as perceived by the potential retiree.

The solution is to treat Bram's proposal - the investigation - as a way of life. In other words, learning and exploring is the best way to avoid boredom. The study can be in any subject and level. An investigation is basically the application and integration of our knowledge with the knowledge we accumulate during the inquiry. A self-unassisted investigation is not always possible; sometimes, an expert should chart the path. Still, there is no greater pleasure than the pleasure of inquiry.

. . . .

In the face of the deaths of great ideologies, postmodern thinkers believe that all that is left to give life meaning is to explore. Their approach, of course, has no chance of reaching the study of the final and absolute truth because there is no such truth. Nevertheless, there is a contribution to human and personal knowledge in the very act of inquiry.

According to the Bible's authors, god justifies the death penalty for eating from the tree of knowledge: "For God knows that when you eat from it your eyes will be opened, and you will be like God knowing good and evil."

LEARNING TO BEAT BOREDOM

Primal humans never ceased to study. Their natural environment provided a never-ending source of useful information. The beetle footprints they spotted on top of the prey footprints could tell them that the prey footprints were too old to follow if they knew that a particular beetle was nocturnal. Most of the discussions of hunters around the fire at night are of lessons they learned from the recent hunt.

There is nothing like learning to beat boredom. The frequent use of the intellectual ability, the accumulation of knowledge, the feeling of the world slowly unfolding before you, the sense of partnership in the achievements of humans, the feeling of teamwork in the company of people in the same field of interest, and especially the enthusiasm and commitment that follows. All of these increase the intensity of the learning experience, preserve its memory, and give it meaning.

In Latin, the word Ludus - school - has another meaning - play. Now that we have time and do not worry about grades, it is time to play in school.

Knowledge is the basis of all our actions and a very important component of ourselves. This implies that adding knowledge is self-expansion. This is the opportunity to revive old aspirations that were suppressed due to the need to make a living. This is the opportunity to discover and express hidden talents.

The movement to return to school is growing among the retiring community. About 100 adult residential communities in the United States are directly connected to a local college. Their residents live near the college and can participate in all college activities and facilities for a reasonable fee.

Sometimes our area of interest is as clear to us as sunlight, and sometimes it involves a little soul-searching. Our current interest areas are far more random than we think. In many cases, becoming involved in a field makes us interested. How often have we become interested in the culture of a particular country only after visiting it?

There are methods for an orderly search of areas of interest, such as listing what excited us and recording in which field we feel particularly talented. As we have already said, our simulation mechanism is not as developed and accurate as we think. It certainly does not allow us to make a reliable simulation of the issues that may interest us. We have no real experiential recognition of a great variety of subjects. We tend to dismiss options for which we have no information. The best way is to risk a mistake. The price of an error is not high, but the return of success, discovering a new area of interest, can be increased.

In one of the semesters I spent at Tel Aviv University, there was a two-hour gap in the schedule between the two courses I planned to attend. I struggled to find a topic that would interest me to fill the void. Having little choice, I chose a seminar on the archeology of the Beer Sheva Valley (after all, I spent a significant part of my life in the area). Until then, I was only interested in prehistory. To my surprise, this seminar became one of the most interesting I studied.

Diversification of interests is as important as the quantity of knowledge for self-expansion. Marilyn Wes Seventh, a columnist and a playwright, said: "The length of your education is less important than its breadth, and the length of your life is less important than its depth".

In economics, a famous law is The Law of Diminishing Returns. This law is also applicable to the encouragement of diversity in study subjects. From a certain point onwards, the contribution of each lesson to the knowledge of an existing subject diminishes. As we know more about the issue, a growing portion of the information we come across is already known.

Another aspect of diversity is the development of the ability to link topics. For example, those who study literature and archeology can easily establish the similarity between literary interpretation and the work of the archaeologist. The archaeologist reads a story from the partial data found at the archeological site and his general knowledge. A similar action is taken by any person reading a story in which

. . . .

partial data on reality are always presented. The practice of this process constitutes an extensive field in the theory of literature called the theory of interpretation (hermeneutics). It also incorporates elements from a third field, psychology.

In addition to improving the skill and enriching knowledge, learning opens the door to new activities and helps meet people with similar interests.

Actress-comedian Betty Midler said: "Cherish forever what makes you unique, cuz you're really a yawn if it goes". Learning helps us become more interesting people, for ourselves and others.

Once you have re-experienced the world of learning, you will never fear boredom again. The very process of learning increases curiosity, and once you return to school, you will not be able to stop.

Learning is the best training for the brain, which has a feature similar to that of a muscle. The more it is adopted, the more it increases its fitness. Studies show that people who routinely exercise their brains are less likely to have dementia.

The discovery of a large group of asymptomatic Alzheimer's patients has led brain researchers to define people with cognitive reserve. Most people with a cognitive reserve are highly educated, full of interest, and have diversified leisure activities. Researchers recommend creating and maintaining a cognitive reserve through stimulating mental and physical activity and social interaction.

The anatomical perception of the brain has changed a lot in recent years. Today it is clear that the brain's plasticity to form new connections is maintained and even improved with training at a relatively late age.

From Insight to Execution - a Conversation about Courage

To summarize

- Courage lies between fear and irresponsible behavior and results from developing self-control.

- Courage can be divided into physical, emotional, intellectual, and moral.

- Postponing correct action often results unconsciously from a lack of courage.

- Failure is essential for personal development.

What can we do?

- Sometimes, defining something as an experiment can be a way to overcome the fear of failure. In most cases, the price of failure is not as dramatic as it seems at first.

- Learn about courage and try to practice courageous moves.

- Build emotional courage by revealing your feelings to yourself and others.

- Build intellectual courage by speaking your mind.

- Build moral courage by cultivating empathy for others.

'Men occasionally stumble over the truth, but most pick themselves up and hurry off as if nothing had happened.' (Churchill)

Early retirement requires courage. The economic and social consequences of such a decision are extremely significant.

Courage was an essential trait for early humans when hunting large animals. Has our relatively protected life degenerated our natural level of courage?

Aristotle defined courage as residing on an axis between fear and irresponsibility.

Before hearing Aristotle's definition, I concluded that whenever I made a leap in my life, I was acting with a certain degree of irresponsibility. I first felt this when I quit my job to study business abroad, spending most of our residual capital.

Courage is the result of self-control. On the one hand, control is needed to overcome fear. On the other hand, control is required to avoid acting irresponsibly. Self-control can be developed to some extent by training; hence, courage can also be developed by training. Aristotle supports this assumption by saying that courage is a matter of habit.

Courage, as a general trait, can be applied to different areas of behavior. Physical courage is obvious. In addition, there are situations where more abstract types of courage are needed, such as intellectual, emotional, and moral courage.

Courage is a trait that feeds on and nourishes other characteristics. Courage is an element in the 'physical fitness of the mind. Its existence allows us to get the best out of our souls, just as physical fitness will enable us to get the best out of our bodies. As with fitness for all types of courage, you can train. The training principle is like fitness training: start with small daily tasks and move on, if necessary, to more crucial lessons.

Physical courage

Physical courage is a key component of a hunter's lifestyle. The giant cave bear became extinct 15,000 years ago in the Americas due to excessive hunting. At that time, humans used nothing more than a pointed stick to hunt dangerous animals. Humans hunted large animals; animals like elephants do not escape and either stand still or charge. Only with the agricultural revolution did the demand for physical courage disappear from most humans' lives. Today it is mainly the share of firefighters, police, and soldiers. Training is the main means of preparing these forces for the courage required during their work.

It may be that the urge of modern humans to seek thrills, such as in extreme sports, is rooted in the lack of opportunities to experience physical courage.

EMOTIONAL COURAGE

Emotional courage is closely linked to self-awareness. Sometimes we hide our feelings from ourselves. It takes courage to deal with negative emotions, often hidden behind a screen called 'caution.' Suppose we dare to develop the ability to acknowledge our negative emotions, confront ourselves, and accept ourselves as whole and imperfect human beings. In that case, we can feel the existence of emotional courage.

Emotional courage training can be done with the help of expressing emotions in writing to ourselves or, if necessary, orally with the assistance of a good friend or a professional.

INTELLECTUAL COURAGE

We have far more opportunities to experience intellectual courage than physical courage. Intellectual courage is, first and foremost, the courage to raise bold ideas. Then, it takes courage to present them again and again in front of a skeptical, suspicious, hostile, or tired audience.

. . . .

Even academic researchers who are paid to come up with bold ideas often fear the reaction of their peers in the field. There are known cases where researchers published bold ideas only when they retired when their livelihood and promotion were no longer dependent on being within the consensus. Galileo's example is just one of many in which non-consensus ideas have met with physical and not just social sanctions.

The way to develop intellectual courage is to challenge small and less important matters. Ask whether things that have been done in a certain way from time immemorial must continue to be done similarly. This practice has many opportunities, both at work and in private life. The next step is to present the thought and try and apply it to see if it stands the test.

Moral courage

Morality is, in some cases, an expression of control in the face of fear. Fear pushes us to straighten corners and not shake the ship. Moral courage is the ability to continue to believe in and apply moral codes when society resists. Mahatma Gandhi's example of nonviolent resistance showed hundreds of millions of Indians how to defeat the British Empire using only moral courage.

Moral courage can be developed in the same method, physically, emotionally, and intellectually. The technique is to start small. Do not lie to children, do not lie at work, do not betray trust, and reject small moral compromises.

. . . .

Morality is always related to our relationship with others. Therefore, moral courage grows on a substrate of empathy for others. Cultivating understanding and compassion is a means of training towards acquiring moral courage. Thus, the right moral action will occur on a day when moral courage will be needed on more fateful issues.

FAILURE

I wrote the following poem about the courage to fail:

An inaudible screeching of reality
Imperceptible stumbles
Turns that seem to be planned
Invisible wrinkles of chuckle

They all excite me
And I experience the failure
As the head of a village walking upright
In a city that does not know of his existence

And so, with a soul clean
From the residues of my pride
I walk to
The next failure

Fear appears in various masks. Postponing an action repeatedly sometimes stems from fear. Arguments are invented to instill doubt in our ability to achieve a certain thing, only to hide from ourselves a strong fear of failure.

Failures may be an important occurrence in our development. It can be used as a measure of courage. It can teach and forge us if it does not deter us from trying again. Failure does not necessarily result from poor decisions. We need to recognize our inability to control all the parameters that lead to success.

Courage is one of the necessary bridges between thought and execution. Courage allows us to give up what we are for what we can be. It will enable us to live and thrive in the real conditions of life - conditions of uncertainty.

Courage illuminates' uncertainty with a glow of interest and challenge on the path to human authenticity.

Try and enjoy

Courage, success, and failure are embedded in the concept of 'experiment.' An experiment is predefined as a step whose outcome is unknown. Sometimes it is easy to overcome the fear of failure if a step, like retiring from work, is defined as an experiment. An experiment makes it possible to act without closing the option to go back on our decision.

A decision to retire can be reversed if the result does not meet expectations. Although we may pay the price in reduced income and status, it is certainly not a decision of life and death as it seems at first glance.

This rule applies to other steps in life. In fact, life can be defined as an endless array of experiments. As the advertisement for a forgotten product goes - try and enjoy!

Make the experience itself a pleasure. Is that not right for you? Try another.

The following quote is sometimes attributed to Mark Twain: "Twenty years from now, you will be more disappointed by the things you didn't do than by the ones you did do. So throw off the bowlines. Sail away from the safe harbor. Catch the trade winds in your sails. Explore. Dream. Discover.."

Primal Health

To summarize

- A review of societies at the beginning of the 20th century, whose diet was traditional or like that of the primal human, reveals that they were free from cancer, heart disease, diabetes, and autoimmune diseases.

- The difference between health and illness is largely due to diet.

- Low exposure to the sun has created a severe deficiency of vitamin D – a very important vitamin in the body.

- The difference in diet between Western culture and pre-industrial societies is in the dominance of wheat, other grains, sugar, and industrially processed foods and a lack of fat-soluble vitamins A, D, E, and K2.

- Humans underwent two waves of nutritional changes: from natural foods to agricultural foods and from agricultural to industrial food: From animal fat to oils such as olive oil at the beginning of agriculture and from olive oil to corn and soy oil produced by an industrialized chemical process.

- 3/4 of the food we consume did not exist during the 2.5 million years in which humans evolved.

- When we are in a state of rest or normal activity, the energy-producing organelles in our body, the mitochondria, prefer fat

- Fat is the preferred energy source for the body, consistent with the primal conditions when food from animal fat was the main energy source, thanks to its abundant availability.

- Plants have evolved toxins to survive. Gluten, found in wheat and other grains, is an example of such a poison. Many people are sensitive to gluten to one degree or another.

- Fruits contain fructose-type sugar, which constitutes 50% of table sugar. Fructose turns into fat and accumulates near the liver. Early humans ate fruit only for a very brief period in late summer.

- Vegetable oils, such as corn, soy, cotton, and safflower suppress the immune system.

- Early humans usually ate once daily, and studies show a health benefit of short-duration fasting.

- The primal human walked for one to five hours a day, ran fast for short distances to escape predators, and lifted objects of various weights.

- Studies show damage to the body from long-duration intense efforts.

. . . .

WHAT CAN WE DO?

- Expose yourself to the sun for a duration commensurate with the latitude in which you live. At 30 degrees, it is for 20 minutes daily in the summer and about an hour in the winter. Or, supplement with vitamin D at 3 to 5,000 units daily. The aim is to achieve a blood level of about 40 to 50 nanograms (ng) per milliliter or, in other units, 200-125 millimoles per milliliter.

- Try to eliminate bread, cakes, pasta, and any other foods containing gluten.

- Avoid consuming vegetable oils except for olive, coconut, and avocado oils.

- Be sure to eat animal fats and organ meats such as the liver.

- Minimize eating fruit and using sugar.

- Exercise, combining intense short-term efforts with long-term, less strenuous efforts 2-3 times a week.

- Fast for 16 hours a day and sometimes for a day or even more.

- Go to sleep when you are tired, and limit light exposure before bed.

Health is where the tragic consequences of our deviation from the initial lifestyle are most conspicuous.

The premise of this book is that humans will function optimally under conditions in which their genetic inventory has evolved over millions of years. On the other hand, they will suffer from adjustment problems if forced to live in different conditions.

For example, in the case of vitamin D deficiency, the studies are mostly consistent with the basic concept of this book. Vitamin D is formed when the skin is exposed to the sun. Presently we spend most of our time between walls. The deficiency in vitamin D turns out to be a partial or complete cause of many diseases of modern times.

Some 70% of the foods in the modern American diet, wheat, corn, seed oils, sugars, and milk, were not consumed during the first 2.5 million years of human evolution and, therefore, can be defined as unnatural for our species. Moreover, seed oils (soy, corn, canola), which form some 21% of the American diet, did not even exist as food 100 years ago, and sugars, which comprise some 15% of the diet, became a commodity with the beginning of the slave trade in the 1500s

SCIENTIFIC RESEARCH ON NUTRITION

In the 1930s, Dr. Weston Price visited dozens of groups that lived on a traditional diet. All of them, without exception, were remarkably healthy. They used knowledge accumulated over thousands of years to deal with problems arising from the dietary change imposed on humans during the transition to agriculture.

The conclusion from Dr. Price's reports is that until not many years ago, we were blessed with traditional knowledge for managing a healthy lifestyle. In the Western world, we have lost traditional frameworks and knowledge. Food supply has been outsourced to profit-driven companies, and health-driven knowledge is no longer accumulated where it is consumed.

Reading scientific articles and studies on nutrition, health, and exercise without basic criteria is a confusing experience. Scientific studies of nutrition are very difficult to perform. They usually have a variety of variables that affect each other, and it is difficult to isolate the influencing factor from the other factors. Therefore, the results are often not consistently repeated. In addition, there is no uniformity in names and concepts. A 'low carb diet' can be defined in one study as a diet where 30% of the calories come from carbohydrates and fat comes from vegetable oil. Another study will give the same name to a diet containing a maximum of 20 grams of carbohydrates, where 80% of the calories come from animal fat.

So how does a person navigate his way in the sea of different studies and interpretations of those studies?

The answer lies in formulating an explicit premise. The question that always remains open is whether the premise is correct.

As most people do, it can be assumed that recognized organizations, such as the NIH and the HMOs, are the final arbitrators. We, the laymen, cannot obtain and understand detailed scientific information. Once we have made such an assumption, life becomes extremely simple, and it remains only to memorize the official guidelines. Perhaps after a while, when we find that the guideline of complete avoidance

. . . .

of sun exposure leads to a deficiency in vitamin D and subsequently to a long list of diseases, we may change this premise.

THE BASIC ASSUMPTIONS OF NUTRITION ARE EVOLUTIONARY

Like all other species, the nutritional requirements of the human species are determined by genes. Genes determine our physiology and morphology. The components of the food we eat activate genes in each cell, and genes determine, for example, which hormones and enzymes will be produced and when. The genes of the animal kingdom, of which we are part, have evolved over billions of years to maximize survival based on the available sources of nutrition. Humans have undergone minor genetic changes in the ten thousand years since the agricultural revolution and especially in the two hundred years since the industrial revolution. They mostly have not affected their basic nutritional requirements. Thus, when human food changed rapidly from the collection of hunter-gatherer food to industrially processed food, a mismatch was created between our genetic structure and the nutritional sources that activate them. Studying the conditions that prevailed when the genetic inventory was formed makes it possible to reconstruct the optimal nutrition for humans today.

EVOLUTIONARY EVIDENCE FOR THE DIET OF HUMANS

To what diet are we best adapted?

I studied for more than twelve years the human diet during human evolution. I read hundreds of scientific papers, published some myself, and obtained a Ph.D. in the subject. I learned that Archaeology can only partly describe the evolutionary dietary regimen. Yes, humans ate everything edible in some places and sometimes, but what was the pattern they adapted to? I concluded that the main part of the answer lies in our body, that is, our physiology, morphology, and genes. The body remembers.

Reviewing many more scientific papers from other fields of science led me to conclude that we evolved into carnivores that specialize in hunting large prey. In zoology, the term hypercarnivore is used for a carnivore that consumes over 70% of its diet from animals. It is the position in the food chain of all social carnivores of large prey. Of course, we consumed plants, but the main physiological and behavioral adaptations were to acquire, prepare, and assimilate meat and fat.

Here are some of the things I found:

Our gut evolved to process and absorb less fiber and more protein and fat. Compared to a chimpanzee, we have a 77% shorter colon, where plant fiber is processed for energy, and 60% longer small intestines, where protein and fat are absorbed.

Our stomach is very acidic, like that of carnivores and scavengers. Acidity takes care of pathogens in meat; therefore, plant eaters have low acidity, and meat eaters have high acidity in the stomach. Maintaining high acidity in the stomach is energetically expensive. It would not have evolved if it were not essential to survival.

The composition of our fat cells is like that of carnivores. Carnivores hold the same amount of fat in many small cells, while omnivores hold fat in fewer larger cells. Humans have more and smaller fat cells than omnivores, which eat more plants.

We nurse our babies for a shorter period, like carnivores. Humans nurse their babies for two years, and chimpanzees nurse for five years. Weaning at an earlier age makes sense when the baby transfers from milk to a diet of protein and fat but not to plant fiber, a very high component of the adult chimpanzee diet.

There are many more pieces of evidence. Most can be found in a paper published in 2021 in the Yearbook of Physical Anthropology (link: https://onlinelibrary.wiley.com/doi/full/10.1002/ajpa.24247).

Here is a summary table of the evidence from that paper:

Biology	
Bioenergetics	Humans had high energetic requirements for a given body mass. They had a shorter time during the day to acquire and consume food. Hunting provides a tenfold higher energetic return per hour than plants, leaving little room for flexibility between the two dietary components. All animals tend to specialize in the highest return items in their niche. For humans, it means specializing in meat and fat so long as they are available.
Diet quality	In primates, a larger brain is associated with high-energy-density food. With the largest brain among primates, humans are likely to have targeted the highest-density food, animal fats, and proteins. Brain size declined during the terminal Pleistocene as humans consumed more plants as they approached agriculture. Diet quality declined at the same time with the increased consumption of plants.
Higher fat reserves	With much higher body fat reserves than primates, humans are uniquely adapted to lengthy fasting. This adaptation may have helped with overcoming the erratic encounter of large prey.
Genetic and metabolic adaptation to a high-fat diet	Humans adapted to higher fat diets, presumably from animals. Study (Swain-Lenz et al., 2019): "suggests that humans shut down regions of the genome to accommodate a high-fat diet while chimpanzees open regions of the genome to accommodate a high-sugar diet."

FADS-Omega3 oils metabolism	Genetic changes in the FADS gene in African humans 85 thousand years ago allowed for a slight increase in the conversion of the plant DHA precursor to DHA. This change may signal late adaptation to a slightly higher plant diet.
Late adaptations to tubers' consumption	Tubers were assumed to be a mainstay of Paleolithic diets that cooking could prepare for consumption. Recent groups that consume high quantities of tubers have specific genetic adaptations to deal with toxins and antinutrients in tubers. It may mean that Paleolithic humans were not well adapted to consuming large amounts of tubers.
Stomach acidity	Higher stomach acidity is found in carnivores to fight meat-borne pathogens. Humans' stomach acidity is even higher than in carnivores, equaling that of scavengers. Adaptation may have evolved to allow large animals' consumption in a central place over days and weeks with pathogen build-up.
Insulin resistance	Humans, like carnivores, have a low physiological (non-pathological) insulin sensitivity. Insulin is released during the consumption of plants.
Gut morphology	Humans' gut morphology and relative size radically differ from chimpanzees' guts. Longer small intestines and shorter large intestines are typical of carnivores' gut morphology and limit humans' ability to extract energy from plants' fiber.
Mastication	The masticatory system size was already reduced in *Homo erectus* two million years ago. The reduced size is compatible with meat and fat consumption.

Cooking	Cooking was hypothesized to have enabled plants' high consumption despite needing a high-quality diet, starting with *Homo erectus*. Other researchers argue that habitual use of fire was evident only around 400 thousand years ago. Fires may have been used for other purposes, such as protection from predation, light, and warmth.
Body morphology	A set of adaptations for endurance running, which is useful in hunting but unnecessary in plat gathering, is already found in *Homo erectus*. Shoulders adapted to spear-throwing in *Homo erectus*.
Fat cells morphology	Human fat cells' morphology is similar to the morphology in carnivores.
Age at weaning	Carnivores wean at a younger age, as do humans. Early weaning *"highlight the emergence of carnivory as a process fundamentally determining human evolution"* (Psouni et al., 2012).
Longevity	Kaplan et al. (2007) hypothesized that a large part of the group depended on experienced hunters for feeding due to their long childhood. Extended longevity in humans evolved to allow utilization of hunting proficiency, which peaks by age 40. The grandmother hypothesis claim women's longevity allowed additional gathering.
Vitamins	The hypothesis for required nutritional diversity to supply vitamins is contested. All vitamins, including vitamin C, appear to be provided in adequate quantities on a carnivorous diet.

Multicopy AMY1 genes	Multi-copies of the AMY1 gene have been hypothesized as adaptive to high-starch diets. However, both findings of its possible lack of functionality and the unclear timing of its appearance limit the use of the evidence to support a change in trophic level.
Archaeology	
Plants	Plants were consumed throughout the Paleolithic, but their relative dietary contribution is difficult to assess from archaeological findings. Recent advances in plant residue identification in dental pluck provide non-quantitative evidence of widespread plant consumption. Division of labor may point to a background level of plant supply. Still, the evidence is based largely on ethnography, which may not be analogous to the Pleistocene.
Stone tools	Stone tools specific to plant food utilization appeared only some 40 thousand years ago. Their prevalence increased just before the appearance of agriculture, signaling increased plant consumption toward the end of the Paleolithic.
Zooarchaeology	First access to large prey, denoting hunting, appears in *Homo erectus* archaeological sites 1.5 million years ago. Humans also hunted large carnivores.
Targeting fat	Humans concentrated on hunting fatty animals at substantial energetic costs. They preferentially brought fatty parts to base camps, hunted fattier prime adults, and exploited bone fat. That behavior may indicate that plants could not have been easily obtained to complete constrained protein consumption.

Stable Isotopes	Nitrogen ^{15}N isotope measurement of human fossil collagen residues has been the most extensively used method for determining trophic levels in the last 50 thousand years. All studies show that humans were highly carnivorous until very late, before the appearance of agriculture. The method has some shortcomings but was able to identify variation in trophic level among present-day traditional groups.
Dental pathology	Dental caries, evidence of substantial consumption of carbohydrates, appeared only some 15 thousand years ago in groups with evidence of high plant food consumption.
Dental wear	Different wear on fossilized teeth as a result of diets can potentially reconstruct diets. However, the claim for the reconstruction of variable diets in Paleolithic humans could not be verified as the comparison of the groups' diets was unclear.
Behavioral adaptations	A comparison of humans' behavior patterns with chimpanzees and social carnivores found that humans have carnivore-like behavior patterns. Food sharing, group-assisted parenting, labor division, and social flexibility are shared carnivorous behaviors.
Others	
Paleontological evidence	Evidence for hunting by *Homo erectus* 1.5 Mya was associated with the extinction of several large carnivores, but not smaller carnivores. This suggests that *Homo erectus* became a member of the large carnivores' guild. The extinction of large carnivores in Europe also coincided with the arrival of humans. Extinctions of large herbivores were associated with humans' presence in Africa and arrival to continents and islands, such as Australia and America, suggesting preferential hunting of large prey.

. . . .

Zoological analogy	Humans were predators of large prey. In carnivores, predation on large prey is exclusively associated with hypercarnivory, i.e., consuming over 70% of the diet from animals.
Ethnography	Trophic level variation in the ethnographic context is frequently mentioned as proof of human trophic level variability during the Paleolithic. However, ecological and technological considerations limit the analogy to the terminal Paleolithic.

What age do hunter-gatherers reach?

Here is a question that frequently arises in conversations about the health effects of the transition from hunter-gatherer life to the present:

"Why should we, living 70-80 years, adapt to a hunter-gatherer diet, whose life expectancy was only 30-40 years?"

The answer is that hunters who have not been preyed upon, have contracted infectious diseases, or have been killed by natural disasters have lived to retirement age. Life expectancy is not a good measure for comparing longevity between societies.

Life expectancy is usually compared at birth. Most of the difference between hunter-gatherers and modern societies is in mortality from birth until puberty. The death rate at birth among hunter-gatherers is about 200 times higher than in the U.S.

Two anthropologists, Michael Gurven and Hillard Kaplan, have found a more scientifically valid measure to compare longevity between societies - a modal age of death. It is the age at which the largest number of people die.

For example, Hadza, a hunter-gatherer tribe living in Tanzania, has a modal death age of 76, with 24% of adults living beyond it. Similar ages and percentages of life beyond the modal age of death have been observed in other hunter-gatherer societies, such as Hache in South America, Aborigines in Australia, and Sun Kung in Africa.

Gurven and Kaplan compared these data to U.S. data in 2002, which are admittedly higher but not by much, given the intensity and quality of U.S. medical service and protection from natural disasters provided by modern living conditions.

An estimate of the magnitude of the effect of the protection from natural hazards can be obtained by comparing the chimpanzees in the wild and in captivity. It turns out that the protection provided by confinement prolongs the modal age at death of chimpanzees almost three times (From 15 to 42). According to these numbers, the protection offered by current living conditions should have tripled our modal age of death. The fact that the extension is only 12% puts a different light on our longevity and points to one or more negative factors that offset the benefit of a protected and padded modern life. Some of these adverse factors will be described below.

Hunter-gatherer societies and even traditional agricultural societies surveyed in the last century did not have heart disease, cancer, or other autoimmune diseases typical of our time. Even tuberculosis, a viral infectious disease very common in the early 20th century, was not known in societies that did not live on the Western diet. However, they did come to contact with western people. Another point to consider is that not only humans but none of the animals that feed on natural foods suffer from the same diseases.

The conclusion is that when we identify the deviation of the Western diet from the traditional diet, we can get important clues to the causes of the diseases of civilization.

WESTON PRICE

One of the great researchers in the field of the effects of the transition from a traditional to a Western diet was a professor of American dentistry named Weston A. Price. Had he lived today, he would surely have been a leading candidate for the Nobel Prize in Medicine.

Prof. Price worked in Cleveland, Ohio, in the first half of the 20th century. He was a sought-after lecturer in dental schools across the United States and the author of dozens of articles and books. He managed the research department of the American Dental Association.

In the early 1930s, after noticing the rapid deterioration of oral health in American children, Price decided to embark with his wife as an aid on a journey to study societies with perfect oral health. He hoped to decipher the secret of dental health by comparing the diets and living conditions of those lucky ones with the diets and living conditions in the United States of his time.

In previous years he conducted research, concluding that oral health is an excellent indicator of general, physical and mental health.

The rumor that traditional societies relatively isolated from the Western world have excellent oral health conditions has directed his travels. From 1931 to 1936, he visited 13 regions worldwide, from the Alps in Switzerland via Africa, Australia, Asia, South America, Alaska, Canada, the Hybrid Islands, and the Pacific Islands. He conducted a very large-scale and thorough study of 27 different groups of natives. Because of his status in dentistry, he has won the cooperation of local health authorities everywhere.

He published his findings from those six years of world tours in a book called Nutrition and Physical Degeneration

Wherever Prof. Price and his wife went, they measured the incidence of tooth decay and the nutritional and general health of the natives. In addition, they took thousands of photographs of the jaw, teeth, and facial structure of members of primitive societies, as he called them, and modern parallel societies.

He conducted extensive laboratory tests to locate the specific components in the diet of healthy people. He identified the main missing elements in the Western diet as fat-soluble vitamins - vitamins A, D, E, and another vitamin he called Factor X.

Factor X was identified several years ago as Vitamin K2. For years he examined samples of butter from all over the United States and the world to identify available sources of the vitamins he had difficulty obtaining. Having managed to gather a sufficient supply of vitamins, he conducted trials on his patients with unprecedented success.

Here is a quote from a summary of his trip to Africa:

"During these journeys in Africa, which covered about 6,000 miles, we came in contact with about thirty different tribes. Special attention was given to the foods, samples of which were obtained for chemical analysis. Over 2,500 negatives were made and developed in the field. If any one impression of our experiences were to be selected as particularly vivid, it would be the contrast between the health and ruggedness of the primitives in general and that of the foreigners who have entered their country. That their superior ruggedness was not racial became evident when through contact with modern civilizations, degenerative processes developed."

According to Price's findings, African tribes had nearly zero percent of caries cases. In contrast, when natives from those tribes partially switch to a Western diet, the percentage rises to an average of 12 percent of the teeth.

Price writes about a group of natives in the Torres Islands between Australia and Papua New Guinea: "In their native state, they have exceedingly little disease. Dr. J. R. Nimmo, the government physician in charge of the supervision of this group, told me in his thirteen years with them he had not seen a single case of malignancy, and had seen only one that he had suspected might be malignancy among the entire four thousand native population. He stated that during this same period, he had operated several dozen malignancies for the white population, which numbers about three hundred. He reported that among the primitive stock other affections requiring surgical interference were rare."

Even looking 70 years back, the scope of Price's research and findings is no less than amazing.

The findings were repeated everywhere he visited. In societies that ate mainly dairy products and fish, the caries rate was close to 0%. In communities whose main food was traditional agriculture, without sugar and flour, the caries rate was low, 1-4%. He did not discover a single society where they did not eat a certain amount of meat or fish. In areas where the Western diet was practiced, tooth decay increased to 25% of the teeth, and up to 50% of the people were infected with at least one tooth. Price found an extreme example among the staff of a small hotel in Guiana in the Belgian Congo. He writes: "This group consisted of the inside and outside servants of a tourist hotel on Lake Kivu. An examination of 320 teeth of ten individuals revealed twenty teeth with caries or 6.3 percent. Significantly, all of these carious teeth were in the mouth of one individual, the cook. The others all boarded themselves and lived on native diets. The cook used European foods."

Throughout the book, the harmful effects of the two products brought by the white man, flour and sugar, are particularly noticeable. The examples of this are innumerable.

. . . .

Flour and sugar were probably the white man's first contributions to the new territories, wherever he went. For the white man to be able to use the natives' lands, he had to provide them with an alternative source of nutrition to that taken from them. This dietary source was primarily flour and sometimes also sugar.

Flour was also the means of payment used by the white man to buy products from places where the money had no value. An interesting example of the connection between flour and tooth decay is given by Price from the island of Tonga in the Pacific Ocean. Tongans were known throughout the Pacific as excellent warriors who never lost a battle. Price reports that their queen's height was 1 meter 88 centimeters (6' 2"). The Tongas were very proud people and believed they were the first creatures created in the world, followed by the pig and the white man in the last place. The Tonga Islands are rich in coconut trees. For several years before Price arrived on the islands, the price of coconut rose quickly. At that time, merchant ships visited the remote islands and paid for the coconut in flour. After a few years, the price of coconut dropped, the merchant ships disappeared, and the flour vanished with them. The number of tooth decay in the inner regions of Tonga, which had never tasted flour and sugar, was 0.6%. Still, the number of tooth decay-infected teeth in the area near the port reached 33%. The more interesting phenomenon was that in most infected teeth, caries was inactive. Price writes: "The temporary rise in tooth decay was apparently directly associated with the calling of trader ships", i.e., the availability of white flour.

In the islands of Torres Straights, the phenomenon of differences in the condition of the teeth and face stood out between populations that lived near the port and between people that lived within the island and were not exposed to flour and sugar. On each such island, the Australian government has set up near the port a shop selling Western goods headed by flour, rice, preserves, and sugar. The profits from these stores were used to maintain the government administrative staff in the area.

Price was able to show that the percentage of tooth decay on each island perfectly matched the time the store was set up. On the island of Badu, the oldest store, the proportion of residents who had tooth decay was 95%. In Murray Island, however, the store was only recently established, and signs of tooth decay were detected in only 12.1% of the population.

Even if Price's findings were reduced to caries, they would be extremely useful. Still, it soon became clear to Price not only the lack of caries he finds in these isolated societies but also the absence of other diseases. The most terrible disease of the 1930s was tuberculosis. In societies that lived on a traditional diet, no tuberculosis was found despite having contact with the white person. What is more amazing and applicable to our generation is that there was neither heart disease nor cancer in those societies.

In his book, Price presents a table that shows the ratio between the content of minerals and vitamins in the traditional group diet and the American diet. For example, in Eskimo, the calcium content is 5.4 times higher than in the American diet.

. . . .

The table clearly shows that the American diet has a severe mineral deficiency relative to the diet of the traditional healthy groups that Price studied.

It can also be deduced from the data in the table that moving away from the lifestyle according to which our body has developed causes a very severe deficiency of fat-soluble vitamins: A, D, E, and K2 of which in the American diet is not even a tenth of the amount found in the diet of healthy societies.

Another conclusion drawn from Price's descriptions is that in places where the food was from plants, humans learned how to neutralize its harmful effects, mainly by soaking, germinating, and fermenting.

The salient conclusion from every page of Price's book is that to be healthy, we must stay as close as possible to the diet by which our body has evolved.

It isn't easy to understand how this simple and logical conclusion, supported by the findings of Price, and many other studies, do not yet constitute the scientific consensus. Most of the scientific world dealing with nutrition still recommends food products that did not exist until a few decades ago or whose industrial processing turns them into foreign foods for the body. Worse, parts of the same establishment, such as the American Heart, Cancer, and Diabetes associations, are participating in a well-funded campaign by influential commercial figures to trash traditional foods.

To those 'trashed' foods, like meat or animal fat, our bodies have adapted in the process of evolution.

ROBERT MCCARRISON - LIFE AND DEATH IN THE HAND OF NUTRITION

Britain had just ended World War One. The British realized that they had virtually no idea during the long war what the ideal diet was to keep their soldiers healthy and fit for combat.

The task of investigating this was entrusted to Major General Sir Robert McCarrison, who was stationed in the Indo-Kush region of northwestern India (now Pakistan) years before when he graduated from medical school. McCarrison noticed during his years of service that the people of one of the local tribes, the Hunza, had almost no illness and lived to extreme old age. He only had opportunities to care for them when they were injured or contracted cataracts in their old age. The Hunza raised goats, cows, fruit trees, and wheat. McCarrison, who linked their health to nutrition, decided to research it.

At the war's end, McCarrison was appointed chief investigator on the issue of the link between nutrition and health. McCarrison settled with his laboratory in Conor in the Madras region of India to scientifically research the nutrition of the healthy tribes of the subcontinent. Its purpose was to compare the diet of the healthy tribes with that of sectors in the Indian population whose health was poor and thus locate the nutrients critical to good health.

. . . .

Following experiments with rats, he chose, besides Hunza, the Sikhs of the Punjab region as models of a healthy diet.

Science relies on comparisons. Ideally, scientific research involves changing one variable, such as diet, and freezing all other variables, such as exercise, sleep, sun exposure, drinking, and dozens of other parameters. Comparing nutrition between groups of people is extremely complex and difficult. Different groups of people live in different conditions from each other in many aspects.

McCarrison thus chose to use Albino rats for his research. Albino rats are widely used in nutrition studies. Rats are omnivores and especially love all types of human food. After all, they have been around us and feeding on our surplus for thousands of years. In addition, they are inexpensive to feed, they breed easily in captivity, and their short lifespan allows us to observe their entire lifespan.

McCarrison began his research with the question: Will a diet of healthy tribes also create healthy rats?

He gave them a diet based on that of the healthy tribes other than fruits.

The rats were also taken out every day to stay outside and be exposed to the sun.

Interestingly, the rats did not have the conditions to maintain physical fitness. They were imprisoned in cages where they could walk carefully but not develop movement at significant acceleration.

1,189 brave rats participated in his first study of the best traditional diet from birth to 27 months, corresponding to

55 years of age in humans. The rats were killed at all ages up to 27 months of age and operated on postmortem to detect diseases that could not be seen without surgery. 1,189 rats are a huge amount relative to modern studies, and it was probably made possible thanks to the availability of dozens of Indian helpers for pennies.

The results, in McCarrison's words, were:

"During the past two and a quarter years, there has been no case of illness in this 'universe' of albino rats, no death from natural causes in the adult stock, and but for a few accidental deaths, no infantile mortality. Both clinically and at post-mortem examination, this stock has been shown to be remarkably free from disease."

Having grounded his thesis that nutrition is most closely linked to health, McCarrison turned to examine the link between nutrition and disease. For this purpose, he took a larger group of 2,243 albino rats. He fed them a diet typical of the lower classes of Madras and Bengal. It is important to note that in all other respects, except diet, the treatment of the groups was the same.

The diet of the lower classes of Madras and Bengal caused rats to get diseases in all parts of the body. McCarrison lists in his article about eighty different diseases, such as heart disease, arterial, lung, cancer, edema, and other forms of inflammation.

Below is the composition of diets:

1. Typical diet of Sikhs / Hunza – Chapati, an Indian flatbread from full low gluten flour, butter, unpasteurized

whole milk, a weekly portion of meat, legumes, carrots, and cabbage.

2.   A typical Madras / Bengali diet - a vegetarian diet that includes rice, legumes, vegetables, spices, and a small amount of milk.

And what about more 'soft' health problems like mood swings and depression?

In another experiment, he examined a typical diet of the 'lower classes of England'. Not only did the rats develop many diseases, but they developed what was commonly called 'nerve weakness' at the time. In McCarrison's words: "They were nervous and apt to bite their attendants; they lived unhappily together, and by the sixtieth day of the experiment, they began to kill and eat the weaker ones amongst them". Remember that the rats did not live in starvation conditions, and only the lack of certain nutrients caused them to change their behavior.

Could it be that the cause of emotional symptoms that we do not tend to define as diseases, such as irritability, is also the result of poor nutrition?

Later, McCarrison confirmed that the Bengalis had a much higher morbidity rate in every illness than Sikhs. For example, Tuberculosis was 280% higher, Cancer was 350% higher, and heart disease was 400% higher, to name a few.

It is also interesting to note that the rate of mental illness in the Bengalis was three times higher than in Punjab.

In conclusion, we have two groups with only one major but very significant difference - nutrition. One led to health, and the other resulted in patients with a wide range of diseases.

And how we address the problem?

Instead of looking for diet as the source, we have set up a huge system of doctors, clinics, hospitals, medicines, and devices to heal dozens of diseases McCarrison has identified. It's hard to believe, but Americans spend an average of $12,000 a year on treating illnesses and only about $8,200 on food!

It seems that the resources that could have contributed to improving our diet for better health are wasted trying to fight every disease out of the dozens of conditions malnutrition causes.

A CHANGE IN EATING HABITS

The aging process of our body takes place at an increasing rate. Aging between 50 and 60 is much faster than that between 40 and 50. When the body becomes more vulnerable at retirement age and does not tend to forgive as in the past, the importance of learning and applying good nutrition increases.

HEALTH AND NUTRITION ARE FIRST-RATE EMOTIONAL ISSUES

The importance of nutrition information we receive as children stems from their vitality to our existence. Our brain is programmed to accept and adhere to instructions from our parents regarding food. For the first two years, the children have no feeling of disgust, and they will touch and eat everything, including their secretions. During this time, they learn from their parents what they can eat.

Elizabeth Cashdan, an anthropologist who noticed that children over two tend not to try new foods, concluded that anything that is not allowed becomes forbidden in their eyes. It also makes sense - there is no way to teach children the thousands of types of foods that are dangerous by negation, and the only way is to learn what is proper to eat.

In this situation, it is no wonder that following a diet different than what your parents ate is difficult.

A typical sense of human omnipotence, combined with bad science and tons of commercial interests, causes us to put daily into our bodies nutrients that have no resemblance to those we have consumed for millions of years. As described, Prof. Price found in 1930 that flour causes enormous damage to health, but this is just one component of the typical Western diet, which our ancestors never ate. Prof. Price was not exactly anonymous in the United States at the time. Still, the establishment's disregard for it continued for many years.

Nowadays, a hunter-gatherer in a home kitchen will not identify almost any food product. Bread, for example, will not be identified by him as food. Likewise, he won't recognize processed vegetable oils such as corn oil, soybean, and canola as legitimate food. The vegetables in the fridge will not be familiar to him at all. Most of them did not come from Africa - his continent, and those of African descent differ greatly in their size and sweetness from their natural state. The last milk he drank was when he was a baby and originated in his mother's breasts and not from cows, sheep, or goats. Equally, he will also not be familiar with all dairy products like butter, yogurt, cream, and cheese. All the artificial drinks we buy, like cola, sweetened juices, and wine, will surely look to him like stale water that is not fit for drinking. He will be surprised to see the sugar, salt, rice, legumes, pasta, flour, breakfast cereals, snacks, chocolate, and dozens of other processed foods that inhabit our kitchens.

The changes in our food happened in two waves. In the first about ten to five thousand years ago, wheat, rice, corn, and dairy products were added. The second, the industrial wave that has been taking place for the past decades, brings us a great variety of processed foods.

What does such a radical change in diet mean?

The Food and Agriculture Organization of the United Nations has found that Americans get three-quarters of their calories from food the primal human was unfamiliar with.

Nutrient-rich foods like meat, eggs, nuts, vegetables, fruits, and fish have previously provided foods. Today they compose only 20% of a typical diet.

ANIMAL FAT

At rest, the body consumes 66% of its energy from fat and 34% from carbohydrates and proteins. Only in extreme exertion, when the health of the body takes on secondary importance compared to the need for rapid movement, does the body use mostly carbohydrates to create energy. There is a resemblance to a car, which burns fuel at a sub-optimal level while working the engine at high revs.

Why are we guided to eat twice as many carbs as fats? Consuming fat accidentally got associated with arterial occlusion. The influential professor Ansel Keys, looked for a link between the percentage of saturated fat in the average diet in different countries and heart disease. He was determined to prove his theory about the connection between heart disease and saturated fats. His determination increased when European researchers mocked his idea at an important conference on the rise in the incidence of heart disease held in Europe.

The data he had from twenty-two countries did not show a link between eating saturated fats and heart disease. He presented in his study only the seven countries that fit his theory. It is difficult to define such an act as bad science - the more correct definition is fraud. But until the fact that he distorted data was proven, it took root in our perceived reality. To this day, quotes from Keys' research can be found in sources of information that teach people to avoid eating saturated fat. Other scientists have shown, for example, that it is possible to choose seven other countries from the same 22 countries and come to the opposite conclusion. France and Switzerland are examples of countries where high fat intake is associated with low levels of heart disease.

Our body stores excess food (including excess carbohydrates) in the form of saturated fat in the fat cells.

This is the body's way of fulfilling its energy needs throughout the day between meals. When we eat carbohydrates, the level of insulin in the blood rises. Insulin diverts glucose (the carbohydrate product) from the blood to the cells. The liver converts the excess glucose to saturated fat. Insulin also stores fat in fat cells. Once the blood sugar and insulin levels drop, the fat returns from the fat cells to the arteries to nourish the body's cells with energy. Is it conceivable that evolution causes fat to flow for long periods during the day in our arteries and cause harm? Is it conceivable that evolution would choose to use fat (mostly saturated) as the body's main energy source at rest if it is harmful to the body?

A full dose of conceit is needed for a scientist to determine that one of the most basic substances the body produces, stores, and carries in its arteries is harmful to it and that oils produced in a chemical process - vegetable oils - are healthy.

Professor Loren Cordain reviewed the typical diet of dozens of hunter-gatherer groups studied in the 20th century. He found that the composition of the fats they consumed was 48% saturated fat, 42% monounsaturated fat, and 10% polyunsaturated fat. In other words, the main fat humans have always eaten in a non-industrial environment is saturated fat.

A study by prominent nutrition scientists Volek and Feinman found that high saturated fat in the blood results from a high-carbohydrate diet (which the liver converts into fat) and not from a high-fat diet. Volek and Feinman concluded that you are not what you eat, but you are what your body does with what you eat.

Despite publications of scientific studies today proving the positive effect of animal fat intake on heart health, 'fake truths' assimilated over so many years are dying very slowly.

A 2020 review of the scientific literature by Astrup et al. regarding saturated fat found that: "Most recent meta-analyses of randomized trials and observational studies found no beneficial effects of reducing saturated fat intake on cardiovascular disease and total mortality, and instead found protective effects against stroke."

Readers of this book are certainly not surprised by this conclusion. Fat, as a source of energy, also stands the top test of the book. The body's preference for fat is evolutionary.

PLANTS DO NOT WANT TO BE EATEN

The idea that there are healthy plants, whose whole purpose of existence is to serve as food for humans and that burst into the sound of grinding our jaws, is typical of our view of humans as the center of creation.

The reality is more bitter. No one, including plants, wants to be eaten.

Plants subsist on solar energy and nutrients from the soil, and animals feed on plants or other animals. The survival process is war - animals against plants, plants against animals, animals against animals - all possible combinations.

The main point is that plants, unlike animals, cannot escape. Most plants have found a defensive solution: Poison!

Almost every plant in nature has several toxins. In fact, there is a constant war between plants that develop new toxins and animals that create new means of protection against those toxins. In turn, the plants that managed to make an unknown toxin and the animals that managed to develop protection against this toxin survive. This is also why animals usually do not eat a varied diet. They have been able to build immunity to a limited number of toxins.

The best proof of toxins in certain plants, which our bodies are not built to deal with, is the need for cooking. If we eat a potato without cooking it first, we will be in danger, and the same goes for uncooked legumes. Cooking neutralizes some toxins; sometimes, additional treatment, such as soaking, fermenting, or germinating, is needed to neutralize most toxins but not all.

Some foods contain toxins that will not necessarily kill us immediately but nonetheless cause us harm. These toxins are usually in a chemical group called lectins. Lectins are proteins that tend to bind to receptors located on the cell walls of our body. They can change the rate of cell division to which they connect or cause it to adhere to neighboring cells and otherwise alter the cell's biochemical activity. Some lectins can be neutralized by various chemical and physical processes. According to Price, primitive societies soaked legumes, oats, and wheat before cooking them, a practice we completely neglect.

....

About sixty years after Price's travels, in 1999, the United Nations Health and Food Agency published a book called Fermented Cereals - A Global Perspective which provides fermentation methods for different types of grains. In traditional societies worldwide, the pre-preparation processes take days and even weeks. They include several steps: germination, grinding, boiling, adding enzymes, and fermentation. One would not have expected such labor and time-intensive processes to be practiced if they were not essential for good health.

GLUTEN

An important example of plant poison is the gluten found in wheat, barley, rye, and several other seeds. Cereals and legumes are a group with a high need for protection. Unlike fruits, roots, or tubers, the seeds of grains and legumes are at eye level for most animals and mammals in particular.

Therefore, these plants have developed particularly nasty toxins against mammals. As mentioned, humans overcame many toxins by soaking, fermenting, germinating, or boiling certain legumes and seeds. Still, we do not do this today for grains that contain gluten. Gluten is needed to bake the compressed and sticky bread we love so much. The chapati, the traditional bread of the Indians, was until recently baked from a low-gluten wheat variety, and so are probably most of the breads known as 'flat breads' like pita or pizza.

Raising dough for a long time eliminates a large part of the gluten. This is how the large spaces inside the traditional

French baguette are created. In recent years, with the development of fast dough processing technology, raising has shortened, and the percentage of gluten in bread has increased even more.

In his descriptions of the damage of flour to the teeth and the structure of the jaw, Price included, without knowing it, the damage of gluten contained in it. Today it turns out that the damage from gluten, as Price already believed in seeing the flour damage, is far greater than causing tooth decay.

A pair of researchers, James Barley and Ron Hogan, have published a book called 'Dangerous Kernels' in which they describe studies that show that gluten sensitivity is much more common in the population than the accepted estimate. New research shows that many people in the world may be sensitive to gluten, in the range between celiac and mild sensitivity.

This sweeping sensitivity is caused by several different damage mechanisms that serve the wheat seeds. The first and best known is named WGA Wheat Germ Agglutinin. Our stomach cells are supposed to be replaced every four days because of their constant exposure to an acidic environment. WGA, like gluten, causes the cell growth process to be shortened to twelve hours. It so happens that a cell, which had to reach the gastric membrane, where it handles the absorption of food when it is developed and at full capacity, arrives ready for battle like a two-year-old child. Thus, the process of food absorption is fatally damaged.

. . . .

Another mechanism, which has only recently been discovered, indicates the reason for the beginning of the process leading to autoimmune and other diseases following gluten consumption. It turns out that gluten causes an increase in the production of a substance called zonulin. Zonulin causes the loosening of the tight junctions between the cells lining the digestive tract. The phenomenon is called 'leaking stomach', which has terrible consequences for our health. The gastrointestinal tract is designed to be impermeable to nutrients before digestion.

Foreign proteins in the blood initiate the production of antibodies that may eventually be directed against the body. By the way, zonulin, whose level in the body increases due to gluten consumption, is also responsible for opening the blood barrier in the brain; thus, gluten affects the brain.

For readers of Price's book, this should come as no surprise. The damage of flour to teeth and the ability to absorb vitamins A, E, D, and K2, in the populations, are documented in his book in detail.

It turns out that gluten can reach any part of the body and cause damage, including psoriasis, multiple sclerosis, eczema, irritable bowel syndrome and other intestinal problems, peripheral and central nervous system problems, upper respiratory tract problems, anemia, chronic fatigue, osteoporosis, depression, autism, and attention problems.

Some of the problems may sound familiar to you from the list at the beginning of the chapter as a result of vitamin D deficiency. It is no coincidence because one of the effects of gluten disrupts the body's ability to absorb fat-soluble vitamins, such as vitamin D.

It should be noted that the gluten-sensitivity tests used today based on the detection of antibodies in the blood detect only a small proportion of cases. In many people who are sensitive to gluten, the antibodies remain in the digestive tract and do not reach the blood. There is a test for antibodies in feces, but it is not yet common. Therefore, anyone suffering from any health problem (from headaches through autoimmune diseases, attention deficit disorders to digestive issues) is advised to try a gluten avoidance period of one month, at the end of which they return to consuming gluten for several days to check if there is any sensitivity.

VEGETABLE OILS

Another group of food products that the primal human was not born to digest is the group of vegetable oils extracted from seeds. This group includes soybean oil, corn, canola, sunflower, safflower, and several other oils, which are produced in a chemical process, and contain large amounts of polyunsaturated oils. In contrast, oils derived from fruits such as olive oil, coconut oil, avocado oil, and palm oil are healthy for us. It is interesting to note that these oils contain mostly monounsaturated and saturated oils.

There is a very small amount (3-4%) of polyunsaturated oils in the human body. About half of the oils are monounsaturated (found in animal fat, olive oil, and avocado), and the rest are saturated fats (found in animal fat, coconut oil, and palm oil).

What distinguishes polyunsaturated oils (PUFAs) from other oils in the health context is their tendency to oxidize easily. Also, the tendency of polyunsaturated fat molecules to be curly causes the cell walls in which they are interlocked, along with saturated fats, to be permeable.

Polyunsaturated vegetable oils are known to suppress the immune system. When kidney transplants began, there was a need to prevent the rejection of the transplanted kidney by the body. The solution was to give an infusion of sunflower oil. In treating autoimmune diseases, PUFAs are also used for the same reason - they suppress the immune system.

Excessive suppression of the immune system may lead to a very serious result - cancer! This is not surprising, as a normal immune system recognizes cancer cells as foreign cells and kills them.

The explosive growth in the consumption of industrially produced polyunsaturated fats stands out as one of the obvious candidates for a cause of the health crisis. In the Sydney Diet-Heart Study, the group consuming more seed oil had a 62% higher death rate during the seven-year study than the control group. In another very large, long-term study, The Minnesota Coronary Experiment, the authors point to possible increased mortality risk in the older than 65 years old group. Reviewing the scientific literature, researchers point out that: "Increasing dietary linoleic acid (a PUFA) has been shown to increase oxidized linoleic acid derivatives in a dose-dependent manner in many tissues.

. . . .

These oxidized derivatives, along with other non-cholesterol lipid mediators, have been implicated in the pathogenesis of many diseases, including coronary heart disease, chronic pain, and steatohepatitis." The relative chemical instability of PUFAs and their tendency to oxidize in the body to potentially harmful compounds have directed attention to their potential role in promoting insulin resistance, obesity, cardiovascular and autoimmune diseases, cancer, and diabetes.

In the paint industry, PUFAs are used as the main components in oil paints because they become sticky after exposure to air. They also become sticky and hard in the body after they are oxidized.

Introducing PUFAs into the diet of animals such as cows and pigs has led to obesity, a desirable effect in animal husbandry. Vitamin E supplementation, an antioxidant, solved most short-term health problems but did not solve another problem of these animals - accelerated aging.

A high content of omega-6 oils in PUFAs is another problematic aspect. In hunter-gatherer diets, omega-3 oils to omega-6 oils are about equal. The Western diet's ratio is close to 20:1 in favor of omega 6. Some researchers today attribute some of civilization's diseases to this ratio gap. American cardiologists have begun to measure the content of omega-6 oils in patients' blood routinely.

FRUIT IN SEASON, NOT ALL YEAR ROUND

Another deviation from the hunter-gatherer diet is the large amount and sweetness of fruits in our diet.

A hunter loves fruit when they are ripe. The problem is that if you lack a refrigerator, preserving fruit for a long time is impossible. The result is that hunter-gatherers usually ate fruit for only two to three months, from late summer to early fall, when the fruit ripens.

The energy in the fruit is stored in part in a type of sugar called fructose, and regular sugar contains 50% fructose and 50% glucose. Extremely high fructose content can be found in fruit juices and soft drinks. Their increased consumption is, according to researchers, the main reason for the increase in childhood obesity in the United States.

We have enzymes designed to break down glucose but no enzymes to break down fructose. The body probably does not like a lot of fructose because when it appears in the stomach, it immediately attaches phosphate to it and sends it to the liver for treatment.

Fructose also disrupts the activity of the hormones leptin and ghrelin, which regulate the feeling of satiety and hunger, thereby causing obesity. This feature of fructose provides an advantage for animals like bears that utilize the fruits to accumulate fat for the winter. Still, we, unconcerned about winter shortages, are left with only the desire for fruit and obesity.

Some people are more sensitive than others to fructose. About 40% of Central Europeans are sensitive to fructose, manifested by bloating, diarrhea or constipation, gas, abdominal pain, itchy eyes, fatigue, confusion, and depression.

Paleo, Ketogenic, and Carnivore
diets

When in the late1970s, a Senate committee headed by Senator George McGovern decided to prepare dietary guidelines for the American people, no one guessed what harm it would cause. The U.S. Academy of Sciences opposed the proposed guidelines, warning that a vast experiment is being run on all Americans but was overruled by politicians.

The science journalist Gary Taubes wrote a book, Good Calories Bad Calories, in which he reviewed the chain of events that led to the publication of national dietary guidelines in the U.S. The book includes a historical review of scientific research in nutrition over the past 100 years.

Another notable description of the scientific and political blunder that led to the guidelines appears in the book The Big Fat Surprise by Nina Teichholtz. Teichholts was so shocked by her findings that she established a formal lobbying group in Washington called The Nutrition Coalition to try to cause the guidelines to be based on better science.

A family of evolutionary-guided diets began to appear when the horror stories of the effects of dietary guidelines started to sink in.

In his book Paleodiet, Prof. Loren Cordain recommends a diet that includes meat, fish, vegetables, and fruits (in moderation). It prohibits eating starchy vegetables like potatoes, grains like wheat, and legumes, vegetable oils, and dairy products.

. . . .

Physicians have also published books recommending, with some differences, diets that, maybe unintentionally, match an evolutionary diet. Richard Atkins (Dr. Atkins Diet Revolution) and Michael Eades (Protein Power) are the best-known. For them, eating dairy products is not considered harmful.

Atkins and Eades' diets may lead to a metabolic state known as ketogenic. The ketogenic state is achieved by consuming no more than 20 grams of carbohydrates daily. The positive effects of the ketogenic diet have become one of the most researched subjects in nutrition. A PubMed search provides references to over 4500 papers on the subject. The ketogenic diet is used to reverse diabetics and obesity and treat epilepsy and other neuropathological conditions, including schizophrenia. It is even tested for the attenuation and prevention of cancer.

The strictest evolutionary-guided diet is the Carnivore Diet. The most active proponents of this diet are Dr. Shawn Baker and Dr. Paul Saladino, who published The Carnivore Diet and The Carnivore Code, respectively. As the diet's name implies, animal meat and fat are the exclusive components of this diet. However, Dr. Saladino later changed his recommendations to include fruit and honey.

The incredible anecdotal success of the carnivore diet in ameliorating scores of medical and mental pathological conditions makes it one of the most popular diets on social media. Hopefully, this popularity will encourage scientific research.

Another dietary trend that has an evolutionary background is intermittent fasting. We tend to eat continuously throughout the day, which is a relatively recent pattern. The internalization of food into the body has significant metabolic implications, including the production of hormones and enzymes, which are designed to be released intermittently. Additionally, fasting has positive metabolic implications. Chief among them is autophagy, the recycling of obsolete and damaged proteins in the cells to prevent their harmful accumulation. Since primal humans ate at random intervals ranging from hours to days, evolution relied on fasting between meals to generate autophagy.

Many patterns of intermittent fasting are practiced among proponents. Short fasting of 16 hours a day mimics the preindustrial eating pattern. The periodic introduction of longer fasting, from one day to a week, is also common to mimic evolutionary conditions. The positive effects of fasting have been shown in scientific studies.

I hope this chapter convinced you that the evolutionary premise is useful and merits serious consideration.

EPILOGUE

Many resources can teach us about hunter-gatherers' lives. Still, apart from nutrition, none can point to how relevant they are to our lives and how we can use them as a heuristic to achieve wellbeing. I hope that the book did that part. Yes, it is quite philosophical at times. Still, the complexity of some of the assertions should not deter from the main argument, which is as simple as can be – We are all hunter-gatherers deep inside, living in a world that is very different from the one in which we evolved. The feeling of unease and sometimes incompetence is only natural under the circumstances. However, once we realize our true position, the road is paved for fruitful changes, provided we gather not food this time but courage.

Printed in Great Britain
by Amazon